Colm - Merry Chri

slow
DUBLIN

ANTO HOWARD

PHOTOGRAPHY BY
MARK CHILVERS & RENÉ BRUUN

AFFIRMpress

hardie grant books
MELBOURNE • LONDON

This edition published in 2009 by

Affirm Press
1 Jacksons Road Mulgrave
Vic 3170 Australia
www.affirmpress.com.au

Hardie Grant Books
85 High Street Prahran
Vic 3181 Australia
www.hardiegrant.com.au

National Library of Australia Cataloguing-in-Publication entry

Howard, Anto.
Slow Dublin.
ISBN: 9780980374681 (pbk.)
Slow guides; 3.
Includes index.
Dublin (Ireland)–Guidebooks. Dublin (Ireland)–Description and travel.
914.183504

Designed by D'Fine Creative in conjunction with Sense Design and Stephen Walker
Printed in China by C&C Offset Printing Co., Ltd.

Disclaimer
All reasonable steps were taken – allowing for bad days, personal dramas, distractions and frequent lie-downs – to ensure that all the information in this book is accurate and up-to-date. Apologies if we've missed anything.

People to thank
Barbara Nealon, Tara Kennedy, Fionn Davenport, Paul Ferriter, Dick and Mary Lincoln, JJ, Eric Dempsey, Michelle Darmody and Slow Food Dublin, Nell Regan, Liam and Sarah, Jennifer Keegan, Nicola O'Callaghan, Matilda, Pat Harrington, Sara Flemming, William Brennan, David Herman, Maya Darrington, Albert, Larry McCarthy all at Naomh Barróg, Kaethe Burt O'Dea, Bill Matthews, Éanna Ní Lamhna, and Mike Haslam and everyone at Solearth.

The Author

Anto Howard was born and raised in Blanchardstown, and has spent much of the last 10 years writing about Dublin and Ireland for international travel guides and publications such as Fodor's, the AA and *National Geographic Traveller*. He lives in a little house in the Liberties, where he writes plays, grows tomatoes and apples, and takes his time to…well, just takes his time. He did, of course, miss his deadline but by no more than we had allowed for.

Anto relished researching and writing *Slow Dublin*, which was a welcome break from the 'bigger and better' style of the travel writing industry. He reckons he found out much more about his city by not looking so hard, and he hopes this book will inspire fellow Dubs to get even more out of this unique city.

Aisling Grimley and her daughters Anna Rose, Kate, Eva and Louisa wrote the Small chapter. Peter Soutter provided enormous help researching, advising and keeping Anto sane. Katie Lincoln was a living slow inspiration, and chipped in with some quality ideas and research.

The Photographers

Mark Chilvers specialises in portrait, travel and feature photography, and has been extensively published in more newspapers and magazines than is worth mentioning. His career has taken him on many adventures, although not many quite as slow and satisfying as this one. He currently lives in London and his photographs appear on pages: 16, 23, 24, 35, 38, 42, 50, 60, 70, 73, 74, 76, 79, 80, 86, 94, 97, 100, 105, 107, 117, 118, 123, 132, 137, 141, 145, 149, 152, 163, 164, 173, 176, 179, 181, 190, 204, 207, 209 and 212.

René Bruun is an Irish-born, Dublin-based photographer. He has been photographing his city for nearly two decades, never leaves home without his camera, and has been widely published in various magazines, travel guides and newspapers as well as the National Geographic website. His photographs appear on pages: 12, 28, 41, 53, 55, 56, 64, 90, 114, 128, 158, 168, 193, 196 and 200.

About this Book

Slow Dublin is co-published by Affirm Press and Hardie Grant, two publishers committed to publishing books that 'influence by delight'. It is part of a series that began with guides to Melbourne and Sydney. This is the first Slow Guide outside of Australia, which may or may not have something to do with born and bred Dubliner and co-publisher Martin Hughes, who created the series and lives in Melbourne. He also edited the book and left the office early today complaining of homesickness. The book was proofed by Hayley Cull, and she and Beth Hall skilfully put it together. Lara Morcombe created the rather spiffy index.

The look for the series was designed by Sense Design, refined by Stephen Walker, and further tweaked by Elena Petropoulos and D'fine Creative who put together this book. Gemma Viselli produced the illustrations.

Local

Natural

Traditional

SENSORY

Characteristic

A Slow Start

The Slow Guide is meant as a handbook for getting more out of life. It's for people attracted to the idea of downshifting but who actually like where they work and live – who love the buzz and richness of the city, but don't want to get bogged down in the madness of it all. It's the closest you'll get to a sea change without changing your address and pulling on your wellies.

Locally and globally, we're getting more stressed (according to the World Health Organisation). Much of the blame lies with our accelerated culture, general impatience and preoccupation with doing everything faster. We want more, so work harder and longer to get it. For decades now these pressures have been pushing one another on, faster and faster, until a cyclone of consuming left us all on the brink of exhaustion. And then the global financial crisis blew us away.

An economic slow down isn't nearly as much fun as deciding to decelerate yourself. And perhaps it's too early to talk about silver linings. But difficult times do tend to make life simpler and priorities clearer. Rather than bemoaning the downturn, as long as you can make ends meet, why not embrace the opportunity to recalibrate your life, to start living for today rather than saving and slaving for the future.

Living slow is not about retreating into an unrealistic rose-tinted yesteryear of Aran jumpers or apocryphal rare auld times; rather it's about being more mindful of the way we live today. It's about being unhurried and appreciating the good things we have around us, counting blessings we're normally too distracted to notice.

Adopting a slow approach to life is about arousing the senses, connecting with community, taking comfort in the natural world and living happier and healthier lives. And in these hard-hit times it's about pulling together, sharing a burden, sharing a hope and learning to live with less.

In a sentence, slow is about quality over quantity, pleasure over pressure, and mindfulness over mindlessness. You can't buy slow; in fact, this is a way to savour life without spending so perfect for these tighter times.

I've been greatly encouraged by the enthusiasm for this book from the many Dubliners I've spoken to over the course of a year's research (you didn't expect me to rush it, did you?). People have warmed to the idea of engaging with this old city from a fresh perspective, and of maximising our enjoyment of the place while minimising the damage we cause. Hopefully this book will

The word 'slow' is used 64

help. It's designed to be practical application of slow values for people who love this place.

You won't hear us brag about Dublin being one of the biggest, best and boldest cities in the world because, well let's be honest, it's not. We're not particularly fussed what outsiders think, and won't exaggerate anything to provide a particular impression. Rather, we celebrate Dublin as a wonderful place to live; a city rich in sensory and cultural pleasures, with a unique way of life and a great personality. Is that not enough?

I was born on the northside, studied in the city centre, and now live just south of the Liffey. Dublin has been my universe for most of my life. For years I wrote travel books about other countries and cities; tempted as I was by new places and people, I never doubted where home was. Not necessarily Dublin but in the company of Dubliners. There is something naturally 'slow' or soulful about us; our desire to wring the last drop of enjoyment out of life shapes the character of the city itself.

After a few years living in New York, I returned in 2000 in the middle of a boom that utterly transformed the place. We gained so much but what did we lose? Sleepy Sundays (to consuming) and front gardens (to second cars) for starters. It could be argued – perhaps by someone brutally misquoting Tolstoy for their own purposes – that rich cities are all alike, but each poor city is poor in its own way. Did we lose a little of our character during the boom time? Did Dublin become more like everywhere else, like a little London or a petite Paris? If we lost a little of what made us different, this book is dedicated to reclaiming it.

If one good thing comes out of this downturn, it might just be a new, personal and communal determination to never again be so easily blinded by the trappings of consumerism and to recognise the next time there walks among us an emperor in the nip.

But this book won't try to convince you of anything. It won't criticise things that are wrong (much), but instead celebrate all the things that are right. Rather than by being earnest or dogmatic, I hope the Slow Guide will influence by delight.

And that's the last you'll hear from me. 'We' write the rest of the book. That's partly to engender a sense of community and to reflect how many people contributed. But also so I can claim credit for the bits I didn't write and share the blame if the book is a dismal failure. We hope the Slow Guide hits the mark, arouses your senses, fires your enthusiasm and nurtures your soul, even just a little. Accentuate the positives, connect with Dublin, and do slow down and smell the roses.

Anto Howard

times throughout this book

CHARACTER

WHAT SHAPES DUBLIN AND DUBLINERS

TIME

NATURE

time

AGAINST THE CLOCK

> “**HOLD YOUR HOUR AND HAVE ANOTHER.**”
>
> Brendan Behan

Let's start at the end. The next time you pass a cemetery, consider those who've gone before us, no doubt preoccupied with similar concerns to those that fill our heads today. Compare the weight of their worries with the lightness of their presence on the planet, the endlessness of time and how quickly it passes. If they could have a few more hours, how would they pass them? Rushing to one more meeting? Sitting in traffic fretting about getting to the gym before it closes? Checking their email every 20 minutes? No, if they could have their time again, they'd no doubt spend it differently.

Man eventually captured universal time, and ironically became a slave to it. Nowadays, hundreds of clocks in laboratories around the world keep time accurate to one second within 3000 years. They make it virtually impossible for time to slip away from us again. Or for us to slip away from time. But perhaps those poor souls in the cemetery would think that the best timekeeper is not the clock but the heart, which measures not the *passing* of time but the quality of time we've spent. If it's empty, we need to redouble our efforts to take, share and lose track of a little time.

Rare Auld Time

Isn't it odd that as we become materially wealthier and technologically more advanced, we seem to have an ever-dwindling supply of time? Technology promised us more time for leisure, but instead strapped us to computers, mobile phones and other gadgets that constantly remind us of the time and the fact that we never have enough of it.

Even the use of that slightly miserly verb 'spend' reminds us of how we see time as a commodity to be accumulated, hoarded and controlled. Is Time something we're constantly pushing against to be more productive, competitive or happy? Or is it the wondrous cycle of the natural world? Does time sound like 'tick-tock' and 'beep-beep', or the dawn chorus of birds singing and nocturnal creatures scurrying? Does it have a little hand and a big hand, or does it look like the changing cloud shadow on the slopes of the Dublin mountains as the sun rises, moves across the sky and sets again?

City life is controlled by mechanical time, we humans by biological time. It's a simple equation and it doesn't fit. These competing clocks cause us to become tense, irritable and unfocused. To counter those negative effects, we have to tune into the natural world more to 'clear our heads'. Perhaps we should focus less on how time should be spent, and more on how it can be savoured.

A good place to start might be reclaiming that old Dublin characteristic of running a little late. It represents a more relaxed attitude to the clock and sets us apart. And its sad and serious decline in recent years is something the slow amongst us should rail against entirely.

The Evolution of a City

Looking at times past helps us get perspective on the present. Peeling back a few of the layers that create the thousand-year story that is Dublin helps form a profile of the evolving city itself. Dublin gets its unique character, after all, not from look-at-me extravagance but a blend of nature, endeavour and time.

EMPTY DUBLIN The north-western view over Dublin from the top of Killiney Hill defies millennia of human inhabitation. Buildings and roads disappear beneath a thick forest of urban trees. It's the perfect location from which to conjure a Dublin before the arrival of mankind: a place of unclimbed mountains, wide, flooding rivers without bridges, and sheets of ancient oak and elm forest filling every inch between. The three huge skeletons of giant Irish elk inside the front door of the Natural History Museum are testament to the kind of creatures that roamed free in those ancient woods, along with ferocious wild boar and graceful red deer.

The first Dubliners didn't arrive until about 7000BC. They may have looked down on the region from a hilltop like Killiney and been impressed with the natural bounty on display.

Get inside their heads with a stiff climb up to the summit of Seefin in the Wicklow Mountains National Park. Here, you'll find a stone-age passage tomb covered with a huge circular cairn, some of the earliest traces of human activity in the region. Few visitors make the trip and there's an inscrutable sadness in the unbridgeable distance between our own age and this partly collapsed monument to a time before time, a Dublin before Dublin.

VIKING DUBLIN If you come up the Liffey on a boat, you'll get a sense of what the Norsemen felt when 60 'Dragon' warships eased their way up the mouth of this strange river to survey the scene in 837. They liked what they saw, returning to throw up a fort on the high ridge where Dublin Castle now stands. The 'Long Stone' or 'Styne' across from the Screen Cinema on D'Olier St marks the site of an original tall stone pillar in what was then a much wider river, a Norse custom to symbolise their possession of the surrounding land. Ireland had its first real town, the network of its narrow streets still tangible in today's Temple Bar.

The Civic Offices known collectively as 'The Bunker' were built at Wood Quay in the 1980s, right on top of Northern Europe's largest urban excavation of a complete, complex Viking neighbourhood. But you don't have to visit the National Museum to see a reminder of Viking Dublin; you might not even have to leave your back garden. The common hedgehog was introduced by the Norsemen as a source of food, and as such marked the start of an Extremely Slow Food movement in Ireland. After catching their hedgehog (a task not to be underestimated) the Vikings spent most of the day just working out how to get around those spines.

GOLDEN AGE

For a sample of Dublin in its Georgian pomp, listen to Handel's *Messiah*: his great oratorio premiered here in the spring of 1742, a reflection of the prestige Dublin held as the second city of the British Empire. It was performed at Neal's Music Hall on Fishamble St, with Handel himself leading the performance from the harpsichord.

Take a short walk during evening rush hour along two Dublin streets: tight, narrow Essex St in Temple Bar followed by broad, grand Fitzwilliam St along Merrion Square. You'll quickly understand the brilliance of Georgian urban planning. The Wide Streets Commission, established in 1757, reshaped the medieval city (sometimes with a ruthless demolition of existing areas) and created vital thoroughfares such as O'Connell St and Bridge, Dame St and College Green.

The Commission led to a property boom that, in contrast to its 21st-century equivalent, was centrally controlled and planned. The Northside was fashionable first; Henrietta St and Mountjoy Square were choice new locations. The Earl of Kildare caused a stir when he built himself a palace on the inferior Southside (now Leinster House) but, as the Earl predicted, the in-crowd followed him across the river and Merrion Square, Stephen's Green and Fitzwilliam Square were soon built to match the finest squares in London.

Stand in the middle of Merrion Square and marvel at the uniformity and planned order of the houses around you – city planning at its finest. But the real genius lay in the fact that while the façades had to be uniform, the interiors behind them could be as varied as the owners required.

VICTORIAN DUBLIN

Strolling through Rathgar or Rathmines reminds us that dark, deep-red brick is the colour of Victorian Dublin (as opposed to the slightly paler Georgian version). These suburbs and others sprung up in the mid-19th century when many of the Protestant and Unionist upper classes moved out of the control of the municipal government after it elected Daniel O'Connell its first Catholic mayor in 150 years.

A trip to Dún Laoghaire on the DART still runs along the path of the country's first railway line, built in 1834 to make this upper-class exodus more comfortable. The launch of the LUAS trams echoes the success of the original tramlines in the 1870s and how they popularised areas like Glasnevin and Drumcondra.

The relative scarcity of Victorian industrial and warehouse architecture in Dublin tells a tale of poverty and imperialism, with native industry positively discouraged as competition to mainland British cities and loyal Belfast. The great exception, of course, was always Guinness, and a stroll through the cobbled canyons between high-walled factories and redbrick storehouses around St James's Gate is a trip through a prosperous past that might have been for the whole city.

Take a closer look at street names in your neighbourhood or the area itself; they often whisper tales of Dublin past. For example, the Tenters, sandwiched between the South Circular Rd and Clanbrassil St, got its name from the once thriving linen-makers who hung their sheets of cloth out to dry in the open air. The artisan cottages on Merchant's Rd in East Wall used to house the workers of the 'Merchant Warehousing Company'

(some of whom were evicted during the 1913 lockout). When burnt lime powder was used to disinfect wooden ships, many of the quicklime stores were housed on Lime St near John Rogerson's Quay.

MODERN DUBLIN With our most recent makeover complete, we might look around us and ask how the last 20 years of development will be remembered and what it will tell historians about us. There are plenty of positives: the wonderful Liffey Boardwalk, the Italian Quarter, the Calatrava-designed Samuel Beckett Bridge, the engineering marvel that is the Port Tunnel, the cleaner Liffey, the spruced-up canal banks, the wonderful LUAS and even the hellish (but possibly necessary) M50.

Although not necessarily slow, these developments show how the city has most recently evolved. They're also a measure of changing attitudes to city living, and our response to the times. We no longer turn our back on Dublin in favour of suburban comforts. We want to commute less and live nearer to work. We want the city to be a place of people and community, not just commerce and government. Alas, a lack of coordination and untrammelled developers' greed has squandered many opportunities, as a walk down the quays will attest.

But the boom years brought at least one wonderful change that will have fascinating repercussions for our little city for many years to come. You only need to stand on Parnell St east of O'Connell St to realise how profound and exciting this particular change is: Dublin has a Chinatown – well, a China street at least. Who would have thought it? Mass immigration and the wonderful diversity it brings will perhaps prove the biggest boon the economic boom gave to Dublin.

Right Here, Write Now

Put yourself in the moment by writing a letter to someone who no longer lives in Dublin. Take the opportunity to go deeper than your general musings and catch-ups over the phone or, eek, email. Include newspaper clippings and 'things' from your life, like favourite food wrappers, ticket stubs and autumn leaves. Keep an eye out for the most ugly, silly or pretentious postcards and send them to friends who'll get the joke.

Remember a time when your mail was about more than admonishing official notifications and tedious marketing tosh? How pleasant to receive something someone has sent with your interests in mind. Generate a little traffic and you'll soon look forward to opening the lid of your mailbox again.

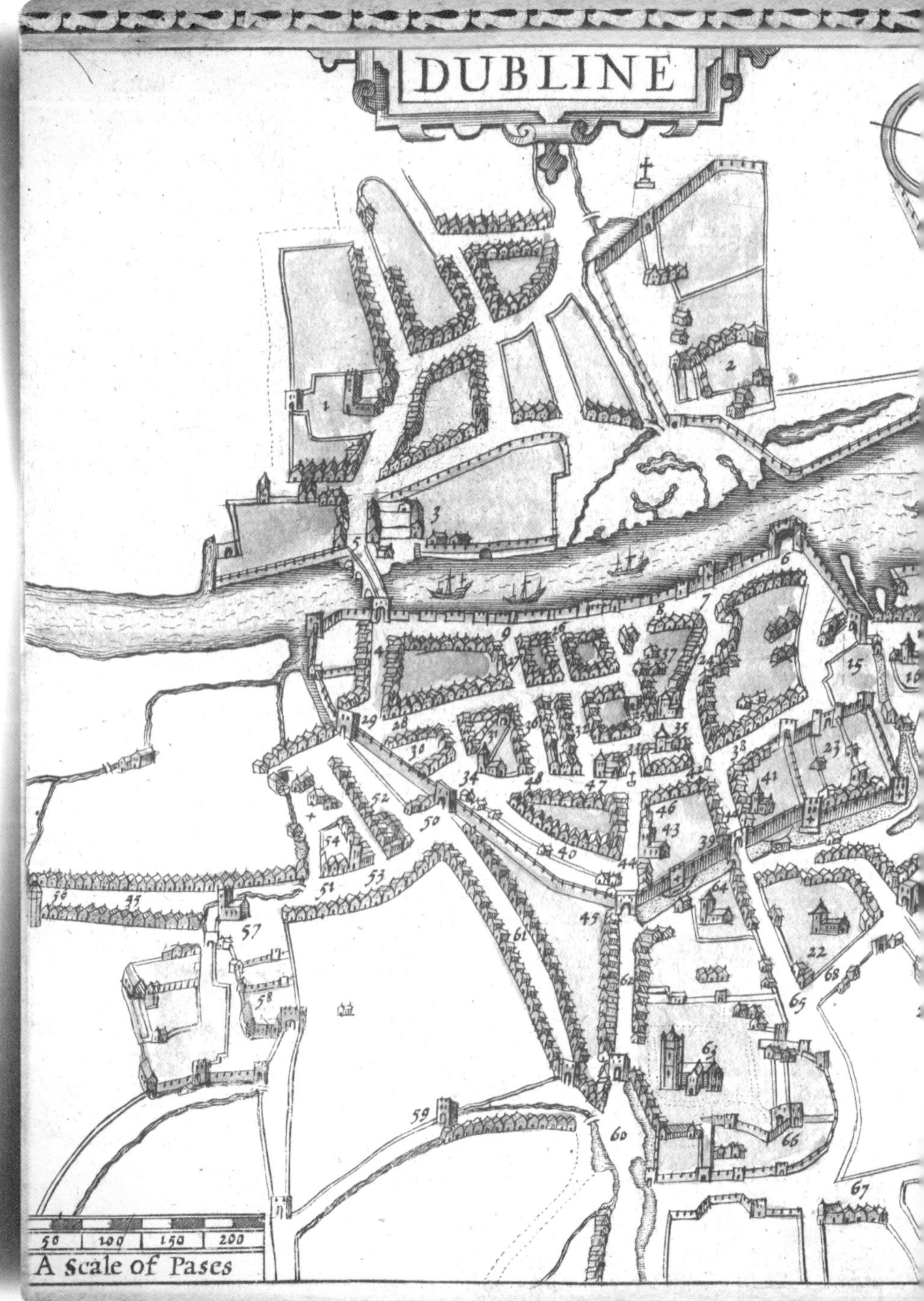
DUBLINE
50 100 150 200
A Scale of Pases

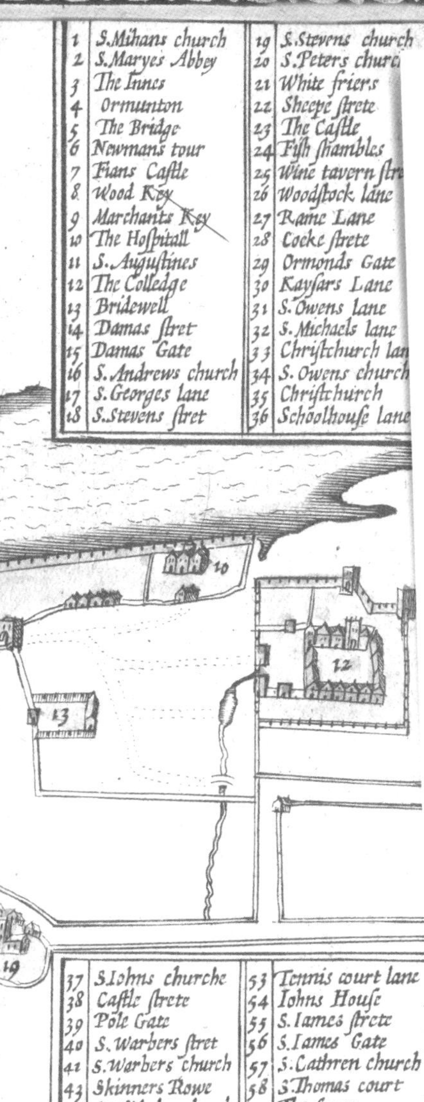

Ye Olde Dublin Tour

The discordantly named John Speed produced the first map of Dublin in 1610, and his sketch forms the basis of our time-travelling tour (with pint). Unlike conventional tours, the object of this one is to tick off the sights you can't see. And all you have to do is look out the window.

Not just any window, mind. The spectacular glass-walled, circular Gravity Bar at the Guinness Storehouse *(St James's Gate; www.guinness-storehouse.com; 408 4800)* is mostly a cramped, noisy tourist trap to be avoided by locals. But there is no better bird's-eye view of Dublin, and if you go there in the slow winter season, particularly in the morning, you might have the place practically to yourself.

Take a seat and get comfortable. Look out the 360° windows and, from atop this temple to modernity, take in the sprawled vastness that is 21st-century *Baile Átha Cliath*. How tiny and fragile Speed's sketched wooden city looks in comparison. Picture the Dublin that Speed mapped in 1610, the result of his great effort reproduced opposite. What would you hear? What would you see? The walled medieval city was pretty much still intact, enclosing a meagre population of 26,000 souls whose numbers had never recovered from the devastation of the Black Death more than 200

years before. So it was a much emptier, quieter place. Sounds of animals – horses, sheep and cows in the fields surrounding the city walls – must have competed with the noise of church bells and workmen on the dock as they met engineless boats sailing up the river to Merchants Quay (number nine on Speed's handy map index). Even delicate birdsong from thousands of nearby trees and hedges may have held sway over much of the city at dawn. And voices would carry far in the stillness: in English and in Irish, the language of conqueror and native, of commerce and home, mixing and blending as the business of a city was transacted. Can you hear it?

Do any names on the map look familiar? Try using these 'survivors' as your guides to re-imagining Dublin circa 1610. Sitting proudly on their high-ground locations, the stone cathedrals of St Patrick's (63) and Christhurch (35) would be recognisable, rising above the rest of the low-rise, wooden city. Trinity College (12) was just 18 years old and consisted of a single small square surrounded by buildings of twinkling new granite. Built well outside the walls on the lands of the once glorious All Hallows monastery (booty in the land-grab of King Henry's Reformation), it would have dominated the otherwise undeveloped southeast bank of the river.

The Liffey, of course, is a constant. But look at how much wider it is at its east end on the map. Much of the land in that area had yet to be reclaimed and the river waters lapped right up as far as modern-day Dame St (14). There was only one bridge ((5), Speed simply calls it 'The Bridge'), at Bridge St (4), so there must have been something of a traffic jam of pedestrians and carts heading in that direction.

The Northside was empty save for a few wooden houses, St Michan's Church (1) and The Innes (3), which still stand today. From your concrete and glass eyrie you can spot the poignant, fractured remnants of the once mighty city wall beside Cornmarket and nearby at St Audeon's Church running along Cook St (28). Here you'll also see the only surviving city gate.

At dusk, plumes of smoke would have filled the sky, rising up from fires in those little houses. And the smell of turf, wood and open-pot cooking would have hung in the fresh air. Take another sip, a gulp even, and let your mind wander. What did they drink? What did they eat? What did they dream of? Are you there yet?

At Any Given Time

DAWN Solitude and sunrises are your reward if you're up before (or stay up later than) everyone else. Anywhere along Dublin Bay is primo for watching the sun rise and slowly turn the black, threatening sea to welcoming blue. **Vico Rock** or **White Rock** in Dalkey are choice locations, especially if you have the nerve to strip off, jump into the bracing water and look along the very line of the sea as the first rays of sunlight appear. Then turn and watch the new light climb up the granite rocks of the cliffs above you.

For another special sunrise, freewheel down deserted **Howth Hill** on a (well-lit) bike as the sun rises over the bay behind you and throws its changing light on the city and the mountains below.

For a city-centre dawn, lean on the side rail of the **Millennium Bridge** facing east and watch the sun come up along the Liffey and creep down the red-brick and granite buildings along the quays. See the shimmering reflection of the elegant white Ha'penny Bridge suddenly appear in the water in front of you, never before looking quite so picturesque. Then wander the city centre and watch Dublin wake.

Smithfield's Wholesale Fruit and Vegetable Market *(St Michan's St; 874 5990)* keeps time to its own beat. Many of the traders are finished work by 10am and enjoy a wind-down drink in one of the early houses dotted around the beautiful Victorian red-brick building. Somehow there is a morning calm among the chaos of the market itself (especially for the non-purchasing voyeur), with the rumble of forklifts on cobblestone and competing smells of flower and onion. Across the road, **Brendan's Cafe** *(Mary's Lane)* is an atmospheric spot for a full and hearty Irish breakfast, or 'dinner' for the traders.

Head to work an hour late and squeeze yourself into the serene and tiny **Bite of Life Cafe** *(55 Patrick St; 454 2949)* across from St Patrick's Cathedral for a green tea. There's no better vantage point from which to watch people rushing to work and, rebelliously, shoot the breeze with the delightful staff here. When the dust has settled on the city, sneak across the road and into the Cathedral itself, empty in its mute splendour, before the tourists arrive. Take a pew. Listen to the silence. Ponder. Laugh.

AFTERNOON Stealing a snooze on the warm, soft grass of a city park in summer is one of life's guiltiest pleasures. Around 2.30pm is the best time, after the lunchtime herd has returned to work. Let the muffled sounds of the city lull you to sleep. Head out to **Dollymount Strand** with this book if you're inspired to go the whole hog; the hollowed-out sand dunes offer shelter from the wind and the sand is feather-soft.

On a wet November day, enjoy the home-made soup and brown bread – free with your ticket – in the cosy, atmospheric little theatre above **Bewley's Cafe** on Grafton St. Dramatic catharsis is a great way to recharge the batteries in the middle of the day. And of course, when you're in need of some mental recuperation, head to a pub where the stained-glass windows turn the sunshine into little rainbows of recreation, for a warm toastie, an early pint and the newspaper (see page 110 in Taste for the best 'toastie' pubs).

TWILIGHT Dublin, with its deliciously drawn-out, shadow-filled northern summer evenings and low buildings, does light better than many cities, and twilight is the magic hour wherever you are.

A particular favourite is to grab some friends and take a place on the perfectly manicured grass outside Trinity College's **Pavilion Bar.** Cold cider seems to work best for half-watching as the cricket game in front of you comes to an anti-climax, accompanied by the sounds of chatter, leather on willow and the occasional clink of bails. Revel in the fact that in modern, confident Dublin the natives can watch and play a 'garrison game' free from all the baggage of imperialist history. After all, a game that always breaks for tea should indeed have a special place in Dublin culture.

NIGHT Go for a walk along the impressive 18th-century **South Wall** of Dublin Harbour and stand in the stillness beside Poolbeg Lighthouse to look back at the great arc of this city-on-a-bay as it lights up for the night. Watch the eerily-lit cargo ships silently pull out of the mouth of Dublin Harbour into the blackness of the open sea and off to the four corners of the earth.

Or, when all the office workers have gone home, take a stroll through the silence of the deserted **docklands.** Dublin's only designated high-rise area is best appreciated in the quietness and darkness of night, when the sound of water in the canal basin carries in the air and the towers of commerce are lit up against the sky. Head back into the city along the Liffey Boardwalk.

Head away from the city lights, to the Phoenix Park or up the mountains, and gaze at the stars and the universe (for all things astronomical see Journey into Space, page 182).

Or, if all that feels like too much exercise, head to an unreconstructed pub and soak up the atmosphere.

A Free Day

Or, just ignore all the suggestions about connecting time and place, and reclaim time as you're own. Spend a day doing nothing except lying in a hammock or sitting in a comfortable chair, listening to the sounds of nature or your favourite vinyl or CD. Turn off your mobile phone and your computer. Remove your watch. Eat cheese and fruit, and drink wine or champagne, savouring their sweet, pungent or spicy tastes as you roll them over your tongue. Take a nap. Read that book. Eat when you are hungry and doze again when sleepy. Play with your children. Play with your dog. Do whatever you feel like, with no timepiece to be your jailer. Feel that time is your own.

ULYSSES
BY
JAMES JOYCE

Slow Icons – Leopold and Molly

"Mr Leopold Bloom ate with relish the inner organs of beasts and fowls. He liked thick giblet soup, nutty gizzards, a stuffed roast heart, liverslices fried with crustcrumbs, fried hencods' roes." From the moment we meet him we learn that Dublin's most famous fictional character was clearly a fan of Slow Food. He shopped locally (the nearby Dlugacz's butcher), cooked at home and took his time over a hearty breakfast.

In fact, should you need *another* guide to slow in Dublin, you could do worse than Joyce's *Ulysses*. The places Leopold and Molly visit (or dream about visiting) map some of the most relaxing and sensory places in the city today: wide and wonderful Sandymount Strand, the stillness and serenity of a cemetery, the cosiness of a classy city-centre pub, and the wild beauty of Howth Head where they first made love under the rhododendrons.

Despite their modest means, they get the most out of their hometown. Like his alter ego Ulysses, Leopold Bloom is an adventurer. His realm is the everyday, the mundane, and he brings a touch of wonder and wit to it all.

He sets out walking the city, as work takes a back seat to life. Haunted by certain ghosts and worries, he employs life's simple pleasures and even chores to pull himself back into the serenity of the present. A bet on the gee gees, feeding Banbury cakes to the birds over the Liffey, enjoying a gorgonzola sandwich and a glass of Burgundy in Davy Byrne's pub on Duke St, smelling the lemon soap he bought for Molly in Sweny's Pharmacy (still there on Lincoln Place) – Leopold knows how to be mindful, slow down and relish the moment. He is perhaps at his slowest when he goes to the outhouse – taking his time over the newspaper which he then recycles as loo paper. He loves music and a good joke, and fills his day with both; there is something quintessentially Dublin about that.

Molly – his languorous, sensual wife – has breakfast in bed. In fact, she spends pretty much the whole of 16 June 1904 in the sack, indulging herself with little or no guilt. She enjoys the sensual side of life and is a master of the wilful fantasy to pass the time.

Her classical alter ego Penelope waits faithfully and worries fitfully over her absent husband – Molly isn't quite so faithful and quickly soothes any worries with a sharp turn of her fantastical mind. When she lets her thoughts run free, no one can stop them; at the time of publication Molly's soliloquy, which finishes the novel, contained the longest sentence in English literature at 4391 words. It ends with the famous declaration of her love for Bloom and her affirmation of life as something to be lived, "yes I said yes I will Yes."

Joyce himself, in a letter to a friend, said that these words indicated "acquiescence and the end of all resistance". Perhaps that is something we can all learn from Molly Bloom – accepting, relishing and reinventing what we have rather than always striving for more. Dublin is a universe if you are an explorer.

nature

KNOWING OUR PLACE

> “ **MAN’S HEART AWAY FROM NATURE BECOMES HARD.** ”
>
> Standing Bear, Ponca Native American

Location, location, location; the Vikings knew a thing or two about real estate. Serene mountains to the south, sheltered bay to the east, open plains to the west and a north watered by three major rivers – the Norsemen would have been drunken fools not to have settled here. But in the hurly-burly of our concrete-and-glass daily life, it can be easy to forget how blessed we are.

Dublin has slowly shaped itself against its unique landscape, the man-made and natural worlds working out an intimate (if not always friendly) coexistence, presenting residents with opportunity aplenty to feel the embrace of Mother Nature. Within little over an hour – the time it takes for many of us to commute to work – we can reach pristine shoreline, isolated hill paths, overgrown river banks and deathly still forests. On a long summer’s day you could comfortably take in all four before sundown, with time left over for a leisurely ninety-nine.

But we can appreciate Dublin’s natural splendour without a day to roam; farsighted Georgian and Victorian planners provided us with countless green, breathing oases in the heart of the city, about 25 per cent of which comprises public parks and gardens. Sometimes just taking a moment to look up can calm a stressed soul, and the flatness of Dublin affords mountain vistas and infinite seascapes perfect for daydreaming.

Unsustainable development might threaten the delicate balance between city and setting, but not even the bulldozers and cranes of the boom could flatten the silent mountains or push back the immutable Irish Sea.

IF YOU NEED A CAPTION, THIS BOOK IS NOT FOR YOU

Seasons

We love to mythologise our bad weather, yet the gap between the statistical truth and the tale of woe can be wider than the mouth of the Liffey. Dublin is actually among the driest counties in Ireland (small comfort, you might say) with half the annual rainfall of our cousins in Galway. In fact, we get only a little more rain than Paris.

Changeability, rather than rain, defines our climate. Sun, cloud and wind never quite follow the script, their capriciousness shaping our lifestyles, playing with our moods and mocking our plans. But the unpredictability has enriched us culturally, made us more adaptable and forced us to create all-weather distractions like the pub. Perhaps part of our character comes from looking out the window of said pub and deciding to laugh rather than cry.

In typically oblique Dublin fashion, we don't have hard and fast rules about when one season begins and another ends. The Celts used the solstices and equinoxes to mark their seasons, which were linked to the growing cycle. We modern Liffeysiders know that seasons change when they decide, and there's no point trying to squeeze them into our neat and compartmentalised calendar universe.

When the seasons do arrive, they provide opportunity aplenty to celebrate how the shifting weather, light and conditions alter the look and feel of the city as well as our mood and behaviour.

SPRING We're restless by the time spring comes, increasingly exasperated by so many false dawns. And then one day we'll be strolling through St Stephen's Green and a sudden, arresting explosion of white, yellow and lilac crocuses around the statue of solemn Lord Ardilaun heralds once again the beginning of Dublin's natural cycle.

Start an argument in your local by suggesting that March and April are the two driest months in Dublin. Statistically you'd be right, but once again the story we tell about the weather is more powerful than any feeble facts, and the story of spring is one of unrelenting, if gentle 'April showers'.

Spring rain tends to catch us unawares, arriving suddenly after a clear sky, psychologically more drenching than the predictably cold, showery days of January. April can be cruel, teasing us with a little hint of summer, then letting us have it with a sudden, dirty shower.

The city, in its natural course, provides for just such an unexpected downpour: the canopy of new leaves on the mature trees that line our older streets and parks offer solid, ready-made shelter. It feels like a very Dublin experience, and truly local character, to meet a complete stranger under a tree for a few moments of shared cloud-movement analysis before one of you throws a jacket awkwardly over your head (spring weather optimists never carry raincoats or umbrellas) and dash out , expletive-heavy, into the weather again.

SUMMER You know it's a warm day in Dublin when the office is empty at half two, workers losing the run of themselves with a hint of sun. A clear morning sky and an optimistic forecast on the radio are all the encouragement we need to change plans and take sudden, renewed interest in the thing called 'work-life balance'.

Take an extra half hour at lunch to enjoy a private picnic or a short snooze in the nearest park, garden, patch of grass or, if all else fails, scorched, flat piece of south-facing concrete. Peel off your shirt, hitch up your skirt and offer that virgin white skin up for a little basting. If you're lucky enough to work near the coast, saunter down to the beaches and swimming holes for an invigorating afternoon dip, even if your wet hair and glowing skin are something of a giveaway back around the water cooler. Any decent boss will understand the need for this annual release of 'climate tension' and turn a blind eye as you sneak out early for an outdoor pint under the evening sun or a spot of very casual river fishing.

Baile Átha Cliath is at its exuberant, carefree best in mid-summer when many take off on holidays. For those left behind this means less traffic, fewer queues and more room along the Grand Canal for a blanket and a bottle of wine with friends. Stolen from time and routine, these impromptu chances to engage with nature, friends and ourselves transform us into a particularly relaxed tribe.

Alas, there's a flipside. As sunshine giveth, the lack of sunshine can taketh away. A protracted bad summer hits the mood like a thump below the belt; the spring leaves our step and patience runs thin. The one saving grace of our crazy weather is our abiding faith that change is just around the corner.

AUTUMN For a sure-fire signal that autumn has arrived, plant a little Virginia creeper at the front of your home. It's that dark green climbing plant you see growing freely across the facades on some of our grandest Georgian and Victorian properties (the east side of St Stephen's Green has a particularly fine stretch) and the occasional mature suburban house. When autumn arrives the creeper changes colour and, with the help of the low-angled light of a late-year sun, turns whole buildings a stunning shade of crimson.

With the return to routine and order, the mood tends towards serenity but remains upbeat. Holidays are over and we turn back towards the city. Days cool down but are still bright and clear. Enjoy the last of the fair weather with an autumn walk through a favourite park that has lots of old trees where you'll be rewarded with a dream leafscape of rich reds and yellows.

To deal with the end of summer and the approaching long nights, a cleverly designed chain of festivals and events leads us, like little stepping stones of pleasure, from the last bout of sunbathing on the beach right up to the bonfires of Halloween. These are not the tourist-trap 'Oirish' festivals of July and August, but solid, meaty sports and local cultural gatherings, including the All-Ireland finals, Culture Night, the Fringe Festival, the Dublin Theatre Festival and the Stranger Than Fiction Film Festival (see page 58). A real autumn pleasure is to don your more fashionable layers and head out to an opening night at the theatre or cinema; it just feels right that it's dark and a little chilly outside when the curtain goes up or the projector flickers on.

WINTER "Conversation about the weather is the last refuge of the unimaginative," said Oscar Wilde, who must have hated Dublin in winter when the time-honoured art of weather-moaning reaches its zenith. We really have two winters: before and after the New Year. It's not that the weather changes – **Met Éireann** *(www.met.ie)* claims December and January are equally wet and cold – but after the pressies have been opened and the empty Baileys bottles tossed in the recycling, the short grey days can seem gloomier.

And that's when our creative complaining gene kicks in. 'Pissing', 'lashing', 'pouring', 'bucketing' – like cursing Eskimos we have evolved a special vocabulary of choice words to the damn the rain. Our shared moaning is a finely tuned, communal coping mechanism to get us through the worst of it – at least that's what we tell the sociologists. Luckily we're not short of great places in which to shelter and complain: the window seat in the chandelier-lit **Long Hall** pub *(51 South Great George's St; 475 1590)* and warm, dusty **Cathach Books** *(10 Duke St; www.rarebooks.ie; 671 8676)* jump out as two prime spots offering cosy respite.

But maybe we can all learn something from the 'Polar Bear' sea swimmers at the Forty Foot and the 'Frostbite' and 'Brass Monkey' winter sailors of Howth who don't just accept the hardy conditions, but revel in them. The next time you're caught in a winter squall, just this once, let it have its way with you. You're already wet so what's the point in worrying? Hear the wind as it howls past your ear, taste the clean, sharp drops on your tongue, feel your hair and clothes stick to your body, watch everyone else dash for cover, laugh out loud at the insignificance of plans. And finally, imagine how much you'll enjoy that warm bath when you get home. Willingly expose yourself to the harshest elements and the rest of the winter will feel like a gentle breeze.

A Dose of Natural Therapy

Maybe because it's in unfashionable Glasnevin, the National Botanic Gardens *(Glasnevin Rd; www.botanicgardens.ie; 837 4388)* is an under-appreciated place for a dose of Mother Nature. Try to arrive just before closing time on a clear day in spring (before the tourist season), when you could well have the 20,000 plant varieties and the 400ft-long greenhouse full of floral exotica pretty much to yourself.

Or bring nature's therapy closer to home by turning your garden into a seasonal gauge with a bit of clever planting. Oaks, elders, silver birch and other trees are veritable havens for wildlife, during their leafy months. Invite birds into your little urban ecosystem by planting spring flowers and juicy autumn hedgerows, and in the winter months, help them out by providing bird tables and nut feeders. While you're getting your hands dirty, remember to leave a few piles of garden waste around to make the hedgehogs feel at home.

Green Spaces

Connecting with nature is physically, creatively and mentally therapeutic. Whether we're deadheading in the garden, strolling through a city park, contemplating the view or even just *thinking* about the great outdoors, nature is just the tonic for our increasingly harried lives. It helps us heal, manage stress, gain perspective, become calmer, see possibilities, feel integrated, focus better, sleep comfortably and even become more neighbourly.

High-density dwelling means our public greenery is now more vital than ever. Even if you work in a windowless dungeon, you only have to incorporate a park, garden or green space into your commute or lunch break to feel healthier and happier. If the Himalayan Alps screensaver isn't working, go for a walk.

PARKS As we love to boast, **Phoenix Park** is officially Europe's largest urban park, but it still retains the carefree feel of the sprawling, slightly disorganised gentleman's estate it once was. We all have our own version of it, but with 1,752 acres, it still has plenty of room for new discoveries.

A bike ride without a destination, randomly choosing left or right along the twisting paths, is a great way to summon some slow serendipity. Deer sightings are almost guaranteed and you may even discover the perfect circular glade near the Pope's Cross where, on the first Sunday of the month, kids from the Smithfield Horse Fair come to chill out, talk horse and let their ponies feed on the juicy grass.

Like many of Dublin's best public spaces, **St Anne's Park** *(Clontarf/Raheny)* was sold cheaply to the city by members of the Guinness family. There is something plaintive about the beautiful long avenue, lined with wind-breaking oaks and pines, that leads from the main gate up to…well, to nowhere. The grand estate house that once stood there burned down in 1943. The 12-acre walled garden, award-winning rose garden, arboretum and restored clock tower are all worth some time.

SECRET GARDENS The slowest green spaces are the empty ones, and we hope mentioning these won't diminish the solitude they offer. Can you call somewhere secret if it's only a four-minute walk from Grafton St? Not prone to exaggeration, Heritage Ireland calls the **Iveagh Gardens** *(Clonmel St)* "the finest and least known of Dublin's parks". Rosarium, rooteries, cascade fountain, woodlands, sunken lawn; this perfectly restored Victorian walled garden does all it can to attract but, miraculously, it is always nearly vacant. Thank God. It's a perfect, city-central place for a little silence, serenity and soft grass. (For stories to impress the kids, see Parks & Playgrounds in the Small chapter.)

And merely a 10-minute walk from O'Connell St, squeezed onto two acres between the old terrace houses of Primrose Ave and Geraldine St, is **Blessington Street Basin**, passed by many and noticed by very few. Built in 1803 as a reservoir (later used exclusively to provide water for the city's whiskey distilleries), it is now just a big old pond ringed by a wonderful tree-lined walk with shaded benches and lots of wild birds.

The Lay of the Land

You can't stop to write a sonnet every time you see the shadow of the clouds move across a forested mountain slope or the rain paint patterns on a still river, but try to find the odd moment to enjoy the topographical magnificence of this city on the bay. Trees, mountains, rivers and the sea, all within a stone's throw – or at least a short bike ride; we are spoiled for opportunity to look up, look out and enjoy.

TREES Go out and hug a tree. Ignore the fact that it's a whopping cliché and give it a lash. Pick something old, gnarly and thick (the native sessile oak will do nicely), something you can't get your arms halfway around. Give it a good squeeze, like an old friend at a wedding. Don't rush; hold it for a minute or two. Rest your cheek against the trunk. Laugh at the fleeting moment of self-consciousness, feel the knots of rough bark under your hands, sense the solidness and life underneath.

Trees are the biggest living things we encounter in our city lives. Mostly we ignore them, or worse, fail to see them in the rush and hustle of our urban universe. But start paying attention and you'll realise, like snails in the garden, trees are everywhere – around 60,000 line our streets alone – and your personal Dublin will be changed for the better. Trees are incredibly generous city dwellers, demanding only a small patch of dirt. In return they provide shelter, shade, adornment, wildlife refuge, fuel, seasonal clock and now, hugging companion.

They are even reliable historians. *'Maireann an chraobh ar an bhfál ach ní mhaireann an lámh a chur'* ('the tree lives longer than the person who planted it') is an old proverb that certainly holds true in the inner suburbs. There you'll find mature trees completely out of scale with the small, terrace-house gardens where they stand, remnants and reminders of a time when the area was parkland belonging to some big-house estate. The 200-year-old-plus walnut and yew trees scattered along Grosvenor Rd in Rathmines are great examples. But even they are veritable blow-ins compared with the mulberry tree in the **Church of Ireland College** grounds *(formerly Rathmines Castle, 96 Upper Rathmines Rd; 497 0033)*. That old fellow has witnessed 350 years and more of Dublin's history, from Cromwell to Bono, and is still going strong.

Native trees hold a particular place in our hearts, popping up in our shared memory, literature and mythology (see box, page 36). The hurls that clash every Sunday at Parnell Park are still made out of native ash, just as they supposedly were for the young Setanta, the mercurial left-corner forward better known as Cúchulainn.

The creators of the early-medieval Celtic Ogham alphabet named each letter after a native tree. More recently, The Dubliners' ballad 'Rocky Road to Dublin' told the story of a hero who "cut a stout blackthorn to banish ghosts and goblins". The blackthorn, the black alder, the trembling poplar, the goat willow, the rowan; even their names sound

Tree Lines

Trees are ubiquitous characters in Irish mythology, associated with a great many tips for a happy life. The rowan or mountain ash is lucky, and will keep witches away if planted near a house or keep a dead man down if planted on his grave. Bring a juniper tree indoors and it will protect you from fire. The elder is not so lucky, cursed by God as the tree Judas hanged himself on. If you clatter a child with an elder stick, you'll permanently stunt their growth. The hawthorn is the fairy tree, so whatever you do don't cut one down lest you want the fairies on your back. They also like holly, which if planted near the house will protect it from lightning. They're not so keen on birch trees so, handy hint, if you don't want the fairies to steal your baby, make the cot of birch wood.

ancient, like a band of medieval druids standing among us. These and the dozen or so other natives managed to adapt to living in modern Dublin, and have even evolved into the perfect Dubliners – revelling in the rain. Taking a little time to get to know the different types, their shape, bark and leaves, connects you not just to some venerable city dwellers but to nature itself. They'll make your next walk to work, to the shops, to the dentist even, that little more fun and uplifting. So when you've finished hugging your first tree, go out and plant another, and make it a native.

The Phoenix Park is the top spot for seeing a good variety of native trees. **The Tree Council of Ireland** *(www.treecouncil.ie)* has a great website for learning what trees are growing where, with activities and workshops for kids. They also list the top 25 trees in Dublin, which makes a wonderful arboreal tour that will take you into corners of the city you might never have visited. It also organises a National Tree Week in spring, a Tree Day in autumn and is altogether a fascinating resource for all things tree-related.

SEA Our urban lives can be very dry; we drive from brick houses along tar roads to concrete workplaces, often living with our backs to the sea and our horizons limited by man-made constructions. Or should that be 'restrictions'?

Even on an otherwise mundane ferry ride to Britain, take a moment to check out the faces of many of the passengers on deck as the ship hits the edge of Dublin Bay and they look back towards home. They seem surprised as they point out the silent cargo ships sliding past them into the huge docks, the kite surfers on North Bull Island or the crazy numbers of wild birds feeding at the sanctuary on Ireland's Eye. It's as if they suddenly realise what it means to live in a bay city, and the profound and beautiful way in which the sea has shaped the character of Dublin.

For most of us, Dublin Bay *is* the sea and the 10km by 7km stretch of relatively calm water is the setting for our sweetest bucket-and-spade memories. Different parts of Dublin have their own beach loyalties (it's the rolling dunes of Dollymount for us) but unless we live on the coast we tend to forget it's there at all. Until something brings us back, kids perhaps, and we're reminded of how it feels to let loose and forget everyday landlubber worries.

Whether we're frolicking along its edge, sailing across its expanse, admiring the view or swimming in its surprisingly temperate waters (8°C warmer than the average at these latitudes), the sea provides glorious relief and the chance to create a new outlook.

And, of course, in the bay are the Dubliners of the underwater world. Grey seals seem to be the friendliest (or most curious) and often come right into shore; they'll pinch fish off your line in Bullock Harbour, and you'll see them while ambling along the East Pier in Dún Laoghaire. The seals actually breed on Dalkey and Lambay islands between September and November, and a quick boat trip to see the multitude with their young cubs is a genuine David Attenborough thrill. The paradoxically *less* common, common seal has a breeding colony on Bull Island.

July to October is the best time to spot both common and bottlenose dolphins, which often ride in the bow wave of boats heading into the harbour. As its local name might suggest, the slightly chubbier harbour porpoise *muc mhara* (or sea pig) has no problems coming close into a busy port like Dublin's, and a glimpse of their black fins undulating across the water is the most *common* wildlife spectacle off our coast.

The much rarer sight of two-metre spouts of water rising into the air will mean a majestic minke whale is paying a visit. They can be seen in the outer bay, sometimes with binoculars from south Bull Wall lighthouse. **Irish Whale and Dolphin Group** *(www.iwdg.ie)* has a great map of sightings around the country.

MOUNTAINS

Around 420 million years ago, the continental plates of North America and Europe collided and buckled to form the range of granite known as the Dublin mountains. Almost as much as the Liffey and the sea, they have shaped the city since man arrived, pushing development out to the west and north.

So influential is this range, that we ignore its official title of the Wicklow Mountains and claim the northern ridges as our own. We're a bit cheeky calling them mountains at all, the highest of the Dublin peaks being Two Rock Mountain at a modest 536m. But ever since humans have walked by the banks of the Liffey, their southern vista has consisted of this granite wall, cloaked in tree, grass and heather, and occasionally capped in snow.

These rugged, wild and sparsely populated highlands are only half an hour from Dublin Castle. Historically this made them a favourite haunt of rebel, bandit and runaway. In the 19th century, to deal with this problem, the British built a military road from Rathfarnham into the most desolate heart of the mountains. Weekend hikers, rafters, climbers and fishermen should give begrudging thanks to the redcoats and their engineers because this is the stunning scenic route we use today.

And just like the outlaws of old, the mountains still symbolise escape. Even if we can't find the time to visit, the sight of them in the distance on a clear day (standing beside St Patrick's Cathedral, for example) reminds us that the world consists of more than concrete, glass and income tax. And they're of course the best place from which to look back on the city, to admire its form, and marvel at the merging of man and nature.

RIVERS Nobody *walks* along a river or canal bank; they stroll. It might be the calming water, or just taking time to notice a group of nesting swans or a particularly fine pussy willow. Luckily, we're never too far from one of these natural, life-enhancing arteries and Dublin City Council lists over 40 watercourses in its domain.

As pub-quiz aficionados know, many are small 'secret rivers' that flow underground: the Poddle, for example, goes subterranean for good at Harold's Cross until it flows into the Liffey through a small grill near Wellington Quay (it once flowed on to form the original moat around Dublin Castle). Most of these smaller streams eventually flow into the big three: the Tolka on the Northside, the Dodder to the south, and of course big daddy Liffey right through the middle.

In our busy minds the Liffey appears as an abstract, slightly brown gap that determines house prices and is crossed on the way from Grafton St to the Ilac Shopping Centre. But a walk up its banks, westward past Chapelizod weir, reminds us that this is a living, moving thing; a thriving and vital part of our urban ecosystem, and a 125km-long source of simple pleasure for the more adventurous spirit. Here the river changes its character and the old Irish name, *An Ruirthech* or 'strong running', makes more sense. The rowing clubs and salmon fishermen at Islandbridge (the grilse run from June to August) know this more vibrant Liffey, where otters and mink reside and vivid blue kingfishers dart.

It's not easy being second, and the Dodder is frequently overlooked, which makes it all the more attractive for a little bit of serenity-seeking or nature-spotting. You can stroll almost the length of the river – from Rathfarnham, through some of Dublin's leafier suburbs, right to the sea. Keep an eye out for jet-black cormorants near Milltown viaduct and grey heron at the Dodder weir.

"Walking along the Dodder takes me out of the mindless grind of city life," says Maya Darrington, riverbank stroller, "straight to the heart of the season and the weather and to a place that seems to be outside time. There is always some new drama to see, whether it is a kingfisher diving from an overhanging branch, a swirling school of fish, a crane poised stock-still in the shallows, swans warming their nests or just the water itself coursing along after heavy rain, all pouring Guinness brown from the mountain soil.

"I start my walk at the Donnybrook end of Herbert Park (near Eglinton Tce), where you have the choice of the paved and tree-lined upper path or the wilder, waterside lower path. If you have a buggy, or are averse to midges or the odd water rat, choose the more civilised upper path. Cross Ballsbridge and follow the river along Beatty's Ave, which looks as if it is still part of a picturesque village, and under the DART line. At Ringsend Rd take the steps at the left hand side of the river and follow the dishevelled path to the breathtakingly vast urban confluence where the Dodder meets the canal basin and the lumbering Liffey," suggests Maya.

Northside suburban growth has taken its toll on some stretches of the 22km Tolka, but it still has some wonderfully serene moments, if we slow down to really notice, particularly along the Botanic Gardens and through from Mulhuddart to Ashtown where pastureland gives way to woodlands, undulating fields and wetlands. (See the Travel and Motion chapters for info on canals.)

Wild Dublin

Éanna Ní Lamhna has a special enthusiasm for creepy-crawlies, and spiders in particular. "We have hundreds of species. And did you know each one makes a unique web design?" she says. "I'm fascinated with them being cannibals. If the males don't bring the right nuptial gift – like a juicy fly – their mates eat them. Fantastic! And you can see all this without leaving your back garden."

Éanna is a local botanist and entomologist, whose humour and earthy, Louth accent on the radio (specifically *Mooney Goes Wild* on RTÉ Radio One) is the voice of nature in Dublin for many of us. Ten years of listening to our questions about robins nesting behind toilet bowls and reported sightings of backyard badgers haven't dampened her passionate belief that we should better integrate nature in our urban lives. "Sure how else would we know it was spring or autumn?" she says, a fair point, emphatically made.

She notes that many of us living in Dublin have rural roots only a generation or two back, so we're still tuned to the natural world and its rhythms, and still crave this in our lives. Her book *Wild Dublin* (O'Brien Press, 2008) is an open invitation to us all to get out and meet our natural neighbours.

The single best place to spot wildlife in Dublin is North Bull Island, Éanna reckons. "Where else in the world can you see a flock of Brent geese so close to the centre of a capital city?" She suggests you grab a handful of the muddy sand and see how it's packed with tiny snails – the Laver spire shell – the key reason so many birds come here to dine. The island's mudflats and saltmarshes attract up to 140 types of wild bird, over 20,000 waders in all. Different species feed on the same stretch of wet sand, and their varied beak lengths (from the pen nib of the ringed plover to the icepick of the curlew) allow them to snail-snack at different depths. Watching a kestrel or majestic peregrine circling the sky and scanning the dunes below is a mesmerising experience. But for Éanna, the biggest treat on North Bull Island is spotting a rare bee orchid, a shockingly pink, yellow and black flower that does a wonderful impression of a nectar-guzzling bee, all the better to fool and attract the real thing. This native perennial flowers in June and July.

Some 24 species of land mammals call Dublin home and many actually thrive on sharing a living space with hordes of Homo sapiens. Éanna celebrates the fact that "Dublin has more foxes per hectare than any other place in the country"; they are great scavengers and lick their chops at much of what we toss in the bin. Does that qualify as recycling? One brave vulpine adventurer has taken up residency at a very prestigious address: No 1 Grafton St, in the garden of the Trinity Provost. He apparently patrols Grafton St at night and has a taste for abandoned hamburgers, chips and the occasional sleepy pigeon.

Another late-night scavenger that hasn't fared so well with our rapid urban expan-

DEER UTD LIMBERING UP IN PHOENIX PARK

sion is the ultra-shy badger. Éanna laments that the M50 is a barrier in keeping "culchie" badgers away from the city ones. "They used to use the old abandoned Harcourt railway line to get about the place," she explains, "but the LUAS put a stop to that." They still use the Royal Canal as a corridor to walk through the sleeping city, and that's the best place to spot them, very early in the morning or late at night. There is also a set in the Phoenix Park.

But sometimes your own back garden is the best place for a close encounter with wildlife. You can encourage birds and insects to visit by supplying bird seed, growing plants that provide them with food and shelter and, of course, by putting a bell on your cat. ENFO *(www.enfo.ie)*, the environmental information website, has great info on what plants attract what birds and animals and how to create a seductive wildlife garden.

Éanna also encourages us to seek out, while we can, an increasingly less-common Dublin sight: the native red squirrel. It may not be with us for much longer. The red squirrel can't match the wily tenacity of its gluttonous grey cousin. A basket of six of the North American creatures was given as a wedding present to a wealthy couple in Castleforbes, County Longford in 1911 and, in less than a hundred years, they have conquered the country including the capital. Notice how they eat acorns before they ripen, gobbling them up before the more discerning red has a chance to feed. St Anne's Park (see Parks in this chapter) is one of the few remaining places to see red squirrels. If you happen to catch a glimpse of them on a fine sunny day in winter, you'll see the low sun light up their beautiful coats.

Bats are another of Éanna's personal favourites and she delights in the fact that Dublin has a very active Bat Conservation Group *(834 7134)*. They use special detectors to pick up their high-pitched signals and record where Dublin's eight species hang out. The group reckons the two canals and the lake in Marlay Park are great bat-spotting locations, but any park or square with trees should do. Night-time from April to November is best for bat-spotting.

Finally, in this short list at least, Éanna has a reward for everybody who's ever turned over a rock to gawk at what crawls out. Most often it's a few ugly, grey, micro-armadillo-like woodlice that thrive in Dublin's damp soil. But one particularly clever species of woodlouse has evolved a special niche for itself here. Éanna has named them 'Protestant woodlice' (certainly a catchier moniker than the official *Androniscus dentiger*) because you'll find them in old churchyards, which tend to be mostly Protestant. Can woodlice distinguish between creeds? The answer to the mystery lies in the ox-blood mortar that was used in the oldest cemeteries, which has become their favourite delicacy.

BE

SLOW DOWN AND SMELL THE ROSES

SEE

HEAR

SMELL

TASTE

TOUCH

see

SITES FOR SORE EYES

> “ **IRISH POETS OPEN YOUR EYES,**
> **EVEN CABRA CAN SURPRISE.** ”
>
> Patrick Kavanagh

Former Dublin resident and poet Patrick Kavanagh began a poem with advice we might take to heart. In the city, sight is our most stimulated sense, and yet the first to fade into the background of our attention. Our eyes are open, but are we actually seeing? Are we looking at anything?

When we really look, we start to see wonder in the mundane. We can become inspired by the little things and see them as microcosmic glimpses of universal truths. Pick up a pebble and picture how it's connected to the universe. Watch how everything changes with the seasons – even just one leaf springing to life, standing proud, changing colour, wilting and letting go. Pick a building you pass every day on your way to work and notice how the light falling on it changes its colour and shade as the year passes from summer to winter. How one sees the world is shaped by our own personality and expectations; so, if we change our perception maybe the whole world will change with us.

Eyes Peeled

Prime yourself for a closer look at Dublin by considering a few local oddities you've probably passed hundreds of times without wondering why on earth they're there.

The best view of the **Guinness Flaking Plant** *(off Victoria Quay)* is from the main thoroughfare through the Phoenix Park as you're heading back into town. This skinny, tall, white, windowless monument to beer-making dominates the view. Besides its austere, industrial beauty, the real wonder of the thing is that it's still standing. Used originally to dry and flake grain, this awkward, abstract structure has been obsolete for years. How did it survive the ravages of tiger economy redevelopment? Apparently it was built out of super-reinforced concrete, and would cost a fortune to tear down. In a city that has lost so many links to an industrial past, let's salute a silent, stubborn giant that has stood firm.

Innocent tourists have been known to mistake it for a piece of daring, if obscure, public sculpture, but the **Old Diving Bell** *(Sir John Rogerson's Quay, close to the Ferryman pub)* is actually the last remnant of a once-mighty diving bell used to take men underwater during the building of the North Wall extension in 1869. Put your hand on the rusty surface and feel the Victorian solidness of the cast iron. Imagine the complete 90-ton monster, which was the size of half a tennis court, being lowered into the water by cables from a floating crane. Men could only work for 30 minutes at a time down there, and bleeding ears and wicked head colds were common complaints.

Depending on your age and the extent of thatch on your roof, you may or may not have noticed the neon wonder that is the infamous, absurdist **Why Go Bald sign** *(George's St, near cnr Dame St)*, erected by Sydney Goldsmith of the Universal Hair & Scalp Clinic in 1962. There is something strangely celebratory and accepting in the grinning face of the chronically bald man as he flashes away, his hair constantly appearing and disappearing again. Every now and then, someone will stop, register it and smile. The sign was rescued from the scrapheap in 1999 by a bunch of loving fans, including Bono (a man who may soon need to avail of the services of the Universal Clinic himself, or possibly already has).

The Cork-born O'Shea siblings were the stone kings of the capital during the 19th century (see the ornate interior of the Museum Building) and they clearly had a messer's sense of humour. Check out their cheeky grotesquery of devilish little **monkeys playing billiards** *(National Library of Ireland, 2 Kildare St)*. The 1860s building was originally home to the Kildare St Gentlemen's Club and a shot of evening billiards was the favourite pastime of its snooty members. Either they were in on the joke, or the O'Shea brothers were making monkeys out of their clients. Similar O'Shea-carved monkeys were removed from the Oxford Museum in the fallout from Darwin's publication *On the Origin of Species*, when the powers that be refused to countenance the notion that man was related to monkey.

Depictions of Dublin

I am the working mother of a very fast two-year-old boy called Liam. For my own sanity I have to frequently position myself in places that ooze slowness. This week had been particularly bad and I'd spent a few days kicking hard against the bustle and demands of the city. I felt like I'd earned the luxury of a wander. So even though it was a drizzly autumn day I pulled on my wellies, Liam hopped into his buggy and we stole one of those precious, agenda-less afternoons ambling about the city encountering 'pictures' together.

I enjoy doing that sometimes, standing silently in front of a work of art. I love the way there's no suggested duration attached to picture contemplating, no ticket, no clock; you come and go as you please. It's one of the gifts of city living, knowing there are clusters of pictures sitting quietly in half-hidden places, waiting for passers-by to encounter. I love the quiet concentration of an empty art gallery. Even exuberant two year olds seem to enjoy the serenity of it.

Liam and I definitely didn't want a plan but needed some sort of a spiritual guide to nudge our wanderings. We settled on the Liffey, that river that runs right through the middle of the **National Gallery** *(Merrion Square West; www.nationalgallery.ie; 661 5133)*. "Oh no it doesn't!" you might pantomime, but just read on as we take a jaunt down the river without ever leaving the confines of the warm, neoclassical building.

There is a nostalgic sadness to William Ashford's **A View of Dublin from Chapelizod** (1795). Christ Church spire and The Royal Hospital in Kilmainham are recognisable, but the traditional landscape shows an almost bucolic, country waterway, flanked by the greens of abundant fields and trees along the bank. The picture resonates with a long lost silence and stillness, and I think of the honking traffic nightmare that Chapelizod became.

Moving down towards the city, **The Four Courts** is an easy-to-miss little watercolour by James Malton from 1793. Despite the title, the image is dominated by the river, and Liam ("Boat! Boat!") and I are fascinated by the sight of people rowing and seemingly going about their daily business. Again a quieter, slower Dublin whispers to us from behind the canvas. Or is this just a day-dreaming artist idolising his subject and overlooking the grime and stink and din of an 18th-century urban centre? Still, you've got to love the idea of commuting rowers on the Liffey. A glimpse of a future Dublin without oil, perhaps?

We hit the city centre with Jack B Yeats' **The Liffey Swim**, arguably the most famous Irish painting of them all. Looking at it again, in the flesh so to speak, makes me realise what I've been missing viewing printed copies; in the thick, textured 1923 work you see his long, paint-laden brushstrokes bring the river to life as it seems in a hurry to get to the sea. He treats the working-class crowd with the same exuberance, his historic move from

SARAH AND LIAM SAVOURING DUBLIN'S "LAST SUPPER"

illustration to expression clear in the way he chaotically captures the jostle and cheer of the quayside locals as they watch the river race, which is still held every August. Dublin life, tradition and fun are captured in those thick, slow strokes.

Liam has had his fill of indoor contemplation and lets me know it's time to get some fresh air. Inspired by the paintings, a trip along the real river becomes our new guide and the Liffey walkway takes us to the child-friendly little square of the Italian Quarter for a steaming hot chocolate. The square is dominated by the huge tongue-in-cheek mural **Dublin's Last Supper** (previous page), a sort of homage to – and joke on – da Vinci's original, and a clever reflection of Dublin humour. Local artist John Byrne chose 13 random people whom he encountered in a day in the capital, accidentally-on-purpose capturing the contemporary cultural mix of the modern, multicultural city. Look closely and you'll see the artist's hand, holding a brush, peeping out from behind a figure to the left and the Four Courts shining in classical arches behind.

On the other side of the river, on the advice of Liam's filmmaker aunt, we seek out the oldest film held at the **IFI Film Archive** *(6 Eustace St; www.irishfilm.ie; 679 5744)*. It's the Lumiere Brothers' 1897 silent, flickering footage of a busy O'Connell Bridge and a rather comical display by the Dublin Fire Brigade in St Stephen's Green. The film was first shown in November of that year for the opening of the Empire Palace Theatre on Dame St, and it feels like a fragile window you could almost climb through into another era.

Our final destination is **IMMA** (see page 54), not quite on the river but it's our tour and we're going with the flow. We're keen to see a more abstract depiction of Dublin. But as we enter the wonderfully green gardens we meet half a dozen cheerful security guards heading home. I'd lost track of time – an entirely pleasant by-product of slow – and the museum is closed. Liam hops out of his buggy and starts jumping about excitedly. He has spotted Barry Flanagan's 10m-high copper rabbit, vigorously beating a drum. There's a warm, wry wit and self-deprecating humour in the big brazen bunny that must qualify as a depiction not of Dublin, but of Dubliners' attitude to the world.

Liam was in heaven, a wholehearted convert to Dublin art.

Sarah Lincoln

Ways to See...

The Mountains

- From the summit of Howth Head with the whole bay laid at your feet and the awkward contours of the Sugar Loaf standing clear against the horizon. Best in winter when the peaks are highlighted with snow.
- Sitting on the left-hand side of a plane flying into Dublin from London as the plane banks for approach and the entire range suddenly looms into view.
- Glimpsed from the city streets in moments that lift you momentarily out of your routine. Looking south down narrow Meath St is a beauty.

The Sea

- Sitting on a rock in an isolated inlet beneath Howth Head with the cliffs looming behind you and nothing but still water in front.
- From Vico Rock, where there's a Caribbean-like view down into the crystal-clear blueness.
- From the halfway point of the Bray to Greystones cliff-walk, looking out on an endless open sea.

The Liffey

- From outside Heuston Station, where sea birds gather and the country river bends and suddenly turns into the city's main artery.
- At the Lucan weir, where the manmade white-water rush hints at the hidden power of the slow old river.
- Along the long, bridgeless stretch between Chapelizod and Strawberry Beds, where the Liffey is at its most secluded, rural and serene.
- At the National Gallery (see page 49).

The City

- Outside the mountaintop Blue Light pub at twilight as the city lights flicker on below.
- Sailing in the bay, where you can sense the full breadth and curve of the city against the shore.
- Swimming at Seapoint with your eyes to the waterline; the city looks like a long and low abstract artwork.

Visual Art

Contemporary culture is a flurry of images trying to convince us things are what they are not. From chemically enhanced fruit to airbrushed models, from advertising to spin, deceiving images dominate our daily lives. One way to see what's really going on is, laterally, through art.

SLOW ART SPACES

The health of our visual art scene can be measured by the presence and quality of artist-run spaces. In Dublin the best studios survive thanks to the tenacity and dextrous accountancy of a few artists' groups. They're not cold, white and intimidating rooms, but living communities that welcome all-comers and pull back the veil that sometimes shrouds contemporary art.

Dublin Culture Night *(www.culturenight.ie)* in late September is an all-doors-open affair where people wander between various studios, meet artists and look over their shoulders to see what they're up to. The wine flows, brushes swish, the chatter never stops and the atmosphere is electric. At other times, you can check out the artist-run **The Market Studios** *(Halston St; www.visitstudios.com; 086 831 8132)* and the not-for-profit **Red-Space** *(2 Rutland Pl; www.redspace.cc)* and support spaces that support local artists.

The **Irish Museum of Modern Art** *(IMMA, Royal Hospital Kilmainham; www.imma.ie; 612 9900)* is a jolt of local modernism in the middle of the grand Royal Hospital, itself a masterpiece of Georgian architecture based on Les Invalides in Paris and with large English gardens. The contrast makes for a lovely slow day of strolling and art appreciation. The artist-led exhibitions and activities here give the place a special authenticity and local vibrancy.

It's among the experimental and usually younger local artists that we get the most accurate portrayal of Dublin today, and sense the significance (or insignificance) of contemporary art here. Have no doubt about it; local artists are very much alive in the city among us, taking the bus and struggling to survive.

The spectrum of subjects and media is limited only by their imagination, but a common theme seems to be a dose of self-deprecation. That's a rare thing among artists generally and a local gift or curse depending on your point of view. It's often fleeting events that throw up the most challenging exhibitions. **The Fringe Festival**, **DEAF** *(Dublin Electronic Arts Festival)* and **Darklight** are film or theatre festivals that have risk-taking as their central thrust.

Cutting-edge also features in established galleries, including the **Douglas Hyde Gallery** *(Trinity College; www.douglashydegallery; 896 1116)*, a modernist concrete-and-glass space for local and international exhibitions as well as a lovely, quiet place to sit and think. The **Hugh Lane Gallery** *(Charlemont House, Parnell Square North; www.hughlane.ie; 222 5550)* is more than a century old and still pushing boundaries, with the Sean Scully Gallery worthy of a visit on its own. Sit and swivel on the long wooden bench while slowly taking in his perception-challenging abstract art. Few other rooms in the city could be more amenable to a spot of meditation.

DANGER
2008
RKZ

PUBLIC ART Public art embroiders the city fabric and has a delightful habit of creeping up on us unawares, jumping out at us one day as we're just going about our business. Juxtaposition of city function and art message is often one of the more interesting results. Rowan Gillespie's moving, disturbing **Famine** sculptures (left) sit at the foot of the temples to international capitalism of the IFSC. The six overstretched, gaunt figures drag themselves down Custom House Quay towards the docks and the escape of a coffin ship.

A Map to Care comprises some 600 trees planted in very-concrete Ballymun. Artist Jochen Gurz asked locals, "If a tree could speak for you, what would it say?" The responses were placed on plaques at the foot of the trees; most express hopes for the future or remember a moment or person from the past, while some are just spur-of-the moment whims. To wander around Ballymun locating them is a slow treasure hunt, and it's warming to imagine how this singularly positive act will continue to inspire as the trees grow.

By its nature, public art is a constantly changing phenomenon and **Artfinder** *(www.blackletter.ie)* is a clever art map created by the Blackletter artists' initiative, which plots ephemeral art projects and happenings around the city. Stick a virtual pin in and go see some art. You might be seduced into a change of perspective or inspired to create something yourself; at the very least, you'll take the pulse of local culture.

Regular public art displays can also be seen at the **Botanic Gardens** and **Iveagh Gardens**, both of which host contemporary outdoor sculptures in summer, combining the pleasures of art and nature.

CINEMA A friend of ours used to love cooking himself a hot dinner and sneaking it into the Stella next door so he could watch the latest release with his broccoli and spuds. Unfortunately, the Stella, the last of the 'local' cinemas, closed its doors for good in 2004. Going to the flicks – a beloved local pastime since James Joyce opened The Volta on Mary St in 1909 – has now become a commuter experience with 'megaplexes' located in large shopping malls. We are shuffled through the loud, hectic, supersize-me shopping and bar areas before finally arriving at an anodyne, could-be-anywhere-in-the-world Screen 19 to see whatever homogeneous fare is on offer, or to be dazzled by the latest CGI effects.

The old **Screen Cinema** *(D'Olier St; www.omniplex.ie; 0818 300 301)* is one of the last picture houses with personality. There are about 30 leisurely steps from street to seat, and the friendly girl who sells you your ticket will probably be the same one who dishes up your popcorn. It's a smooth operation that eliminates queues and stress; on a dry evening you can sit outside on the little raised cobbled area and wait for showtime.

Another slow spin on cinema is to seek out Irish films. The **IFI** *(6 Eustace St; www.ifi.ie; 679 5744)* lacks the charm of the Screen but is the spiritual home of local filmmakers and the only place where you can see older and rarer copies of long-forgotten Irish gems.

The low-budget, do-it-yourself vibe of digital film makes **Darklight** *(late June; www.darklight.ie)* a great place to seek out avant-garde filmmakers and their unique (and often strange) depictions of Dublin and Dubliners. It provides opportunity aplenty to challenge visual assumptions about the city.

THEATRE Dublin has a unique affinity with the stage of course, and throughout history our playwrights have poked and prodded the public consciousness and riled the establishment to such an extent that riots seemed to become the norm there for a spell – with JM Synge's *Playboy of the Western World* and Sean O'Casey's *The Plough and the Stars* the most famous examples.

Both of those took place at the **Abbey** *(26 Lower Abbey St; www.abbeytheatre.ie; 878 7222)*, now very much part of the establishment. It is still a place for a long and luxurious night at the theatre, but to find the dramatists taking risks and holding a mirror up to contemporary society we have to look elsewhere. Or listen; each Autumn, the **Dublin Theatre Festival** *(www.dublintheatrefestival.com)* is a public conversation on national identity and the changing nature of theatre itself.

One new direction it's taking is the sight-specific movement that showcases Dublin itself as a lead character. The focus is often on humorous visual feasts of colour and movement that take audiences to everyday parts of the city that are suddenly altered and refracted in a whole new, hyper-real light. **The Dublin Fringe Festival** *(second two weeks in September; www.fringefest.com)* has been at the forefront of this experiment, its OuterSpace venues popping up all over the city and disappearing almost as quickly.Performance venues have included the public toilets in St Stephen's Green, a hotel bedroom on the quays, a gay bar on Talbot St, a derelic school in Ballymun and in the water at the Grand Canal Dock – the Fringe Festival has opened up the whole city to performance.

FESTIVALS Dublin went so festival-mad over the last decade, that a week without a festival became cause for celebration. Some are thinly disguised tourist traps but there's also a bunch of authentic local events that celebrate local character and encourage us to mingle.

The Festival of World Cultures *(last weekend in August; www.festivalofworldcultures.com)*, at venues throughout Dún Laoghaire, has become as much a celebration of the changing face of Dublin as an introduction to international culture. It's a three day creative bender of exotic colour and exuberance.

Calling it the **Festival of Light** *(last Sunday in November; www.dublincity.ie)* might be a stretch, but it's the simplicity and tradition of the annual switching-on of the city's Christmas lights that makes the event such a pleasure. For decades it has signalled the beginning of the festive season; the shiny Dublin Fire Brigade Band marches down O'Connell St accompanied by a slightly chaotic and brightly coloured gang of dancers, stilt walkers, lantern carriers and inner-city kids having the craic. The lord mayor flips the switch, illuminating the 18m Norwegian spruce and sending ripples of light through the city centre as adjoining streets and over 4000 shops light up.

But our favourite festivals are the unpretentious affairs organised by local communities stoking civic pride; the bottom-up events are a great inspiration to visit parts of the city you would otherwise never pass through.

Chapelizod *(late June – early July)*, **Howth** *(mid-July)* and **Fatima Mansions** *(August)* have three of the more vibrant and varied, but a leisurely search online will unearth a whole lot more. Start with the Irish Festival Guide *(www.irishfestivalguide.net)*.

Or you might prefer to just start your own; all it takes is a few fearless people with a bit of energy and flair. Approaching local councils and media outlets is a good way to harness support and even raise a few bob.

Glass Man Harry

The next time the priest's sermon drags on and your gaze wanders out the window, you'll wish you were in a church adorned with the beautiful stained glass of local lad Harry Clarke (1889–1931). Perhaps better known for his work as a book illustrator, Clarke was, as they say, a dab hand with the auld stained glass, his work adorning churches in Terenure, Donabate, Castleknock, Balbriggan and a UCD chapel.

Clarke's windows are distinguished by the finesse of his drawing, which you've probably admired at that *other* local temple (since desecrated), Bewley's on Grafton St. But our favourite Harry Clarke experience is a visit to St Joseph's Church (Terenure), when the afternoon sun is streaming through *The Crucifixion and Adoration of the Cross*.

Clarke died of TB at the tender age of 42, after suffering continuous bad health, probably not helped by the toxic chemicals he worked with. Talk about suffering for your art.

Colours of Dublin

Brick **red** in Dublin is the colour of class: lighter, mottled almost-pink is Georgian posh, while darker crimson of 19th-century terrace housing identifies workers' enclaves. **Silver-flecked grey** Wicklow granite signals authority and gravitas, from the hallowed halls of Trinity to the hot-air chambers of government buildings and the bullet-pecked walls of the old GPO. Countless shades of **green** hint at the city's hidden natural world: the fern green in the Botanic Gardens hot-houses; the sea green (or "snot green" as Joyce preferred) waters off Sandymount Strand in June; the forest green of over 20km of wildlife-packed hedgerows still inside the city boundaries; the yellow green of a Cavan Sugarcane or Ross Non Pareil native apple sold in the Temple Bar Market. But for every tint of green, the city matches it with a **blue**, like the cornflower blue of the water at Vico Rock in summer; the sapphire of a just-after-twilight sky over the Dublin mountains; and the sky blue and navy of the Dubs blowing another Croke Park semi-final in August.

MY CITY

Stop, Look up, Stare

How much have you really considered Dublin's architecture? Most of us pass the same buildings so many times without really noticing them that we eventually suppose they hold nothing of interest. But reflecting on the why, what and when of our built environment helps to connect us with our surroundings.

Mike Haslam of the Dublin ecological architects, Solearth, took us on a slow tour of his favourite Dublin buildings and styles. We joined him on the north–south, cross-city route he walks to work each day.

You can usually find at least one man-made structure to fascinate and delight on even the most mundane of journeys. It doesn't have to be a show-off, headline-grabbing edifice. Keep a lookout for more discreet, typically Dublin constructions that appeal to more than one sense and alter with time and light. "You have to be open to it," says Mike, "but time, season and mood can suddenly make you aware of your built surroundings in a beautiful and modest way.

"I live just beside the **Blessington Street Basin**, so I often begin my mornings looking out onto that almost-Venetian urban water space and watching the heron that has grown up there," Mike says of the little urban oasis that is a combination of the industrial and natural.

He heads down **Fontenoy St** where there's "a neat line of uniquely Dublin Victorian terrace houses". Paradoxically, the street's sweet and melodic name – which was chosen while Ireland was still held firmly in the bosom of Empire – refers to a nasty 1745 battle in Belgium when the French-led Irish Brigade actually gave the Brits a pasting. "The blood-red brick of these houses is as much the colour of Dublin as the lighter, more celebrated Georgian variety," Mike suggests.

The houses were built as workers' cottages for employees of the old Broadstone Station and canal interchange, and the area is hemmed in on four sides, giving it a close-knit, working-class village feel. But what excites Mike every morning is the unusual house shape: a generous one storey with high ceilings on the front dropping down to two storeys at the back. He almost rhapsodises when describing how this low street-level facade "opens up this powerful vista of a broad skyscape with the red houses against it, that's very unusual for a street this width. I haven't seen it any other place except Dublin." We like to think that James Joyce, who lived at number 44 for a while, pondered on this beautiful skyscape as he penned his infamously erotic 'Fontenoy Street Letters' to his absent, unshockable Nora.

From the best of Victorian Dublin, Mike's morning commute takes him onto **Henrietta St**, his favourite, unheralded stretch of Georgian terrace. "It's thankfully underdeveloped and even a little shabby," says Mike, "but at certain times of the day when the light is bouncing off the cobbles onto the front of the buildings, the street can be breathtaking." Bemoaning the perfect, dull uniformity of the recent faux-Georgian facades that blight whole sections of the city (especially the quays), Mike delights in the imperfections and variations in colour and texture of the handmade bricks along the street. "We often got the leftovers from British brickmakers," he explains. Mixed with the wear and tear of time, this very human imperfection gives Dublin's Georgian houses their particular mottled look that plays so well against the northern sunlight. Mike points out the intricate **King's Inns** ensemble standing proud and slightly incongruous; it's the smallest of James Gandon's neoclassical public buildings in the city. Splendid Henrietta St was built during a construction boom driven by a newly confident and increasingly wealthy city. Sound familiar? How many of the buildings put up in the last 20 years will age as elegantly as these?

Before he crosses the river Mike sometimes stops for coffee in the 2003 **Quartière Bloom**, or Italian Quarter, on the north side of Millennium Bridge. This is one piece of Tiger construction that really "works with the city". Rebellious, football-crazy, anti-war and always-quotable developer Mick Wallace famously stated, "If you build shite in an area, the area will stay shite." Determined to avoid that fate, Wallace combined his love for the communal squares of Italian cities with local character. And it works. Mike reckons it "fits in with the modesty of scale of the old Georgian houses that were on the quays". The narrow lane slows you down and calms you before opening up onto the vibrant shared space of a busy little square of restaurants. The apartments are low enough to be part of the buzzing space, which Mike contrasts to the foundering development of Smithfield Square where the tall apartment blocks remove any human contact with those below. Without people, without faces, buildings can very easily turn into walls.

Better, Mike reckons, is the restored 1892 **Smithfield Fruit Market** *(St Michan's St)*. It's an impressive industrial building – something we are short of in Dublin – with the subdued light, large interior scale and melding of steel, brick, stone and glass. But what makes it a special stroll for Mike is that "it's full of people going about their business; there's a natural theatre about it". Commercial spaces often lack this drama, this action that doesn't require you to participate or to spend any money if you don't want to; the space itself is completely unobtrusive.

Though a few yards off his direct route, Mike waxes lyrical about the masterpiece of city planning and design that is **Trinity College**, which grew organically since Queen Elizabeth signed its charter in 1592 and displays different epochs in its construction. "The buildings serve the spaces generously," says Mike, and though we don't think of Dublin as a city of squares, Trinity is full of them. There is a very tactile and visual change of character from "the granite formality of the Front Square to the more relaxed grass and brick of the squares near the back and the playing fields".

He nominates the 1853 **Museum Building** as "an especially sensorial space, a wonderful fusion of industrial Victorian processes and slow artisan craft". What looks like a

UNFAMILIAR? THE GPO IN FLOOD

striking line of tall chimneys stretching up over the building "aren't chimneys at all," says Mike, "but a years-before-its-time ventilation system by which the building recovers lost heat".

So advanced was this design that it was used as a model for Temple Bar's eco-friendly, low-emission **Green Building** *(15–19 Essex St West)*. When this sustainable residential building was constructed in 1994 it was seen as something very much beyond the mainstream, showcasing now more common building technologies like underground heating and wind turbines on the roof (the second of these nearly caused the building to crack and they now serve as 'kinetic sculptures', meaning they are no longer turned on).

Coming to **Temple Bar**, Mike is reluctant to jump on the bandwagon of slagging it off as a developer-driven nightmare. "Cities are dynamic, you can't stop them changing." He admires "gathering spaces" like **Meeting House Square**, while pointing out the harsh, slightly arrogant clash of styles and scales of the surrounding buildings. "They're all crying out, 'look at me!' Temple Bar as a whole failed to create a village atmosphere because there was simply no room to breathe."

Mike compares this to a very defined, organic village area, the **Liberties**, mostly built to house Guinness workers. "The simple palette of materials is what makes the old Dublin working-class areas special. The houses are actually quite austere," Mike notes, a line of smooth red brick with almost no ornamentation. That's what makes the window boxes and brightly coloured doors so important; they are the signs of individuality played out against a communal setting, "spaces for people to add their own charm".

Mike's final destination, his working place, is the beautifully serene and environmentally innovative **Daintree Building** *(Pleasants Place)*, which he and his partner Brian designed. Completed in 2005 as an "ecological and holistic living complex," the actual brief from the owner – who runs the charming paper shop at the front – was for "a green oasis in the city, with the smell of coffee and baking bread in the morning". The Cake Cafe (see page 106) provides the olfactory dimension and the intimate courtyard's buzz of work and play. They worked with an artist to create the now wonderfully overgrown green gantry, decorated with used CDs, bicycle pedals and other bric-a-brac, and laid sedum grass on the barrel-vaulted roof for drainage.

They wanted a building that would in fact show its years and age gracefully, so they used particular materials including Donegal western red cedar, a local lime render and copper cladding. The cedar already has a silver tinge and the copper is tarnished and turning green. Again Mike was drawn to a "multi-sensorial" experience, with even the natural paints, oils and waxes providing a faint citrus smell. The building is "far from perfect" as Mike concedes, but even so, it may be a beacon for future Dublin planning.

hear

LISTEN TO DUBLIN

> **“ DON’T UNDERESTIMATE THE VALUE OF DOING NOTHING, OF JUST GOING ALONG, LISTENING TO ALL THE THINGS YOU CAN’T HEAR, AND NOT BOTHERING. ”**
>
> Winnie the Pooh

The blackbird’s whistle has been a reliable harbinger of spring in Dublin since time immemorial. But these days, how are we supposed to hear the songbird’s message over the clamour of city acoustics and the incessant bloody beeping of our own gadgets? Dublin City Council bylaws define noise as “unwanted sound”, and life in the city comes with a daily ear-bashing of car alarms, kango hammers, text beeps and jet engines. Dubliners aren’t as quick to blow the car horn as the denizens of other cities, but this polite patience is fading as our life constantly speeds up. Noise and speed seem to be intimately related, our need to squeeze more out of every second upping the volume of impatience and desperation.

But beneath this hubbub lies a much more subtle soundscape, the distinct rhythms and riffs of Dublin. They add to a sensual fabric that distinguishes Dublin from anywhere else on the planet, day from night, one season from another, even one street to the next. Even the mighty sea and howling wind are silent unless you open your ears to the whispering tides and rustling leaves. Really listening to what’s going on around us is a good way to understand, appreciate and take care of it, like a master mechanic listening to an engine, or a doctor to your insides. So take a stethoscope to Dublin and make some discoveries of your own.

Schedule of Sound

Forget seeing in the New Year; *hear* it in with the cascading sound of the bells of Christ Church Cathedral at the stroke of midnight. There's no better way to start **January** and your year of living aurally. Listen to the festive chatter of the crowds die away to a frosty hush as the last few seconds of the old year fade away, before the Cathedral Society of Change Ringers herald the New Year as they have since 1670. It's the only time they really let rip, with all 19 bells echoing waves of optimism across the city centre.

Scientists tell us air molecules huddle closer together on a cold day, meaning that sound carries faster and further. Perhaps this is why the cacophony of honks, squawks, barks and quacks that drift in off Bull Island is so incredibly clear along the seashore by the Clontarf Rd and St Anne's Park. Our mild winter (relative to their arctic home, that is) brings large populations of brent geese, wigeon, teal and shoveller ducks, little egret and grey herons to the mudflats of the island, and their joy at the bounty they find is loud and unfettered. Only weeks earlier they would have been lunching with polar bears.

A wicked east or northeast **February** wind clatters horizontal rain onto the glass of the cosy DART as it winds along the wild winter coast. The differing sounds of wind-hurled rain can be heard throughout the city: hammering on the glass bus shelters, bursting on the soaked bark of trees and pattering on the stretched fabric of umbrellas. If you get off the train at Pearse St in the morning and the wind is in the right direction, you might be greeted by the simultaneously discordant and captivating clamour of tuning violins, trumpets, pianos and clarinets as the students of the Royal Irish Academy of Music *(36–38 Westland Row; www.riam.ie)* get ready for a day of lessons and scales.

Rude, animalistic foghorns in Dublin Harbour signal a good day to head indoors to the solitude and whispers of the old section of the National Gallery *(Merrion Square West; www.nationalgallery.ie; 661 5133)* or the sheet of silence that cloaks the National Library *(2/3 Kildare St; www.nli.ie; 603 0200)*, where the rustling turn of a single page carries through the chamber.

Around **March** you'll hear the start of the mating season for the beautiful coots on the pond in Bushy Park. These slate-grey and usually taciturn birds suddenly turn aggressive and noisy with a wide range of crackling, rasping and explosive trumpet calls accompanying the beating of water with wing. Late in the evening they are at their most belligerent and leave you in no doubt about the origins of the phrase, 'mad as a coot'.

Bumblebees often appear on the first sunny day in March, and can be heard reverberating throughout Dublin's flowering bushes, with the exotica of the Botanic Gardens in particular attracting hordes. Their lazy buzz evokes a sense of summer, and keeps us alert and mindful of the moment. Bumblebees themselves have no ears and *feel* sound as vibrated through sound waves and materials.

In parks in **April** – if you can hear beyond the personal trainers geeing up their charges

– listen to the wind rustling the leaves and try to distinguish the sounds made by different trees. Some are very distinct, like the faint whistle of a breeze fluttering the weightless leaves on the bamboo in the garden of the Chester Beatty Library *(Dublin Castle; www.cbl.ie)*. The Phoenix Park, with its abundant and varied species, is nature's mixing desk of wind, bark and leaf. Notice how the soft rustles at this time of year differ to the raspier sounds of the same trees in autumn, when the dry leaves brush and crackle against each other.

Spring is the high season of children's GAA and the thwack of ash on sliothar or thump of leather foot on leather ball is almost drowned out by parents roaring from the sidelines, baiting referees with shouts of "get yourself a pair of effing glasses!".

Mountain rains fill the rivers, amplifying the roar and crash of the weirs along them. Chapelizod, Palmerstown and Lucan are all good locations on the Liffey to hear the rushing water, but the Dodder weir by Rathfarnham Bridge is a more contemplative spot to let this elemental sound flush your mind clear of everyday worries.

Even a car alarm waking you in the wee hours could be a blessing if it has you alert for the magnificent natural symphony of the dawn chorus in **May**. The fantastic *Mooney Goes Wild (RTÉ Radio One, Mon–Fri, 3–4.30pm)* has introduced us to the joys of this early-morning bird opera, but you can hear it anywhere that has a smattering of trees and a bit of cunas.

Niall Hatch of the Dublin branch of BirdWatch Ireland *(www.birdweb.net)* tells us that "each habitat has its own distinctive chorus members". Cabinteely Park, which is maintained by the local council as a wildlife haven, has a particularly good songbird population. Each morning, the robins (sharp, repeated trill), thrushes (chirp and whistle bursts) and blackbirds (fuller, rounder whistle) are first to sing out. Next come the jaunty notes of the tits and lively descending song of the chaffinches. And then all hell breaks loose with the cawing of the rooks and even more aggressive hooded crows. If your luck is really in you might catch something rare, like the abrupt flourish of a Goldcrest, Ireland's smallest bird.

Soaking it in, ponder the wonderful fact that the dawn chorus never ceases, moving across the earth with the early morning light, a wave of eternal melody.

Hear Here

Next time you're in an urban park, close your eyes and cop an earful. Listen to the city din and, in your mind, place it way off in the distance. Tune in to the sounds immediately around you, the natural symphony you normally don't hear. Take a few minutes; listen to your heartbeat, your breathing, the tick of your watch (what are you still doing wearing a watch?). Feeling calm? Now go out and sing, shout, stomp, and laugh out loud at the racket you're making.

CLOP-CLOPPING THROUGH SMITHFIELD ON THE WAY TO THE FAIR

"Four-t'one-the-fave" tempt the bookies along the rails at the Fairyhouse Easter Festival *(www.fairyhouseracecourse.ie; 825 6167)*. Some of the best jump-racing of the year, including the Irish Grand National, is also a feast of ear-warming sounds like the whinnies of excited thoroughbreds in the parade ring, the brush of the birch fences as the field jumps as one, and the low thud of galloping hooves on soft ground as they pass the post. The shrieks of winners, howls of losers and rip of Tote betting slips are never far behind.

The plop and ripple of leaping trout in **June** makes a river walk a wildlife thrill. Along the Dodder from Herbert Park to Beaver Row in Donnybrook is a great stretch to watch and listen, an abundance of flies in warm weather luring the brown trout out of the water for a snack. It all happens so fast that the sound of a fish breaking the surface as it falls back in might be the first you know about it.

A fine day in early summer is best heard on the beach, amid the cry of gulls and the muted crescendo of a wave passing over your head. On a calm stretch of water, float on your back and pick up the pat of children's plastic shovels against wet sand as they perfect lopsided sandcastles along the shore; listen for the comforting rattle of the DART as it rolls by and the iconic, wind-up melody of the whippy van flogging ninety-nines to the sun-stroked masses.

With the faintest wind in **July**, an evening walk around Dún Laoghaire or Howth Harbour will always be accompanied by the unique, tinny beat of parked sailing boats clang-clang-clanging in the water. The melody comes from wire-hard halliard ropes knocking against the hollow aluminium masts, equally evocative of adventure and calm.

The best city buzz in summer is along the Royal Canal where native dragonflies and their smaller cousin, damselflies, feast on midges. With names as pretty as their glimmering bodies, the banded jewelwing and spring redtail dart along the water, their vibrating drone the signature tune of a healthy, oxygen-rich waterway. (If you're interested, the easiest way to tell the difference between a dragon and a damsel is that the dragonfly rests its wings flat like an aeroplane when still, while the damselfly folds its wings back behind its body.)

The clop-clop-clop of city horses on cobblestones peels back the years and hints at a slower, quieter and indeed smellier Dublin. In the busy tourist month of **August**, a lot of inner-city horses earn their keep hauling screeching hen parties and cooing American lovers around St Stephen's Green and beyond. If you find yourself in the Liberties around John Dillon St of an evening, listen for the distinctive rattle of their tired hooves on the old Liberty cobblestones as they return to their secret little stables at the back of their owners' houses for a night's kip.

Bandstands really come into their evocative own when staging summer concerts. But even when empty there's something dreamlike, almost fairytale, about bandstands that makes us feel like we could stand in the middle and just twirl our worries away. They are reminiscent of the Victorian era when brass bands were in vogue, and our favourites are at the bottom of a grassy natural amphitheatre in the Phoenix Park; the perfectly maintained 1887 version in St Stephen's Green; and the exceedingly picturesque bandstand at Herbert Park, which was built in 1907 for the Irish International Exhibition.

An especially hot spell (who are we kidding?) is followed by a reviving summer thunderstorm. Notice the preceding stillness, an electrified moment, when word goes around the increasingly hysterical bird telegraph that it's time to find shelter. From the safety of a good window, enjoy the rumbles and cracks of lightning and afterwards hear the birds again, their chorus relieved and vibrant as they make the most of their newly drenched surroundings.

Back-to-school **September** fills the city with the wild, chattering and atonal outpouring that is 'little break' – 11am each weekday, when pent-up kids spill out of every primary school door and fill the town with a life-affirming racket that is picked up on Geiger counters on the other side of the planet. The big games leading up to the two All-Ireland finals bring a host of boisterous culchie (and we use the term affectionately) accents to the capital, from the lyrical aphorisms of unbeatable Kerry to the straight-talking earthiness of eternal bridesmaids Mayo.

But it's not just footballers going head-to-head in September; this month also brings the mental, autumnal sound of fallow deer bucks rutting in the Phoenix Park. Shocking, primal roars accompany the stamping of hooves and the crisp, fencing clash of antlers. Seeing the uninterested female – the purpose of all this ruckus in the first place – blissfully and silently unaware, enjoying a lush patch of grass, turns this aural action movie into an overblown romantic comedy.

For children **October** is merely a lead up to Halloween, as the rest of us are reminded with the constant thud of bangers and the rasp of wood on concrete as pallets and planks are dragged to secret hiding places. Halloween itself is the wild crackle and hum of bonfires, the rustle of plastic trick-or-treat bags and the twang of elastic bands securing face masks.

On tree-rich streets like Northumberland Rd, notice how the lunchtime pedestrian rush raises the loud, improvised jazz-drummer swish of leaves under our feet as different gaits kick through fallen autumn leaves.

A **November** storm at sea brings the crash and whish of spray as waves hurl against man-made walls in the harbours and along the South Wall. The storms send wide flocks of squawking, complaining seagulls right up the Liffey. And us humans indoors.

There's something particularly reflective about visiting a grand and empty church in winter, and music is a constant element of services at St Patrick's Cathedral *(www.stpatrickscathedral.ie; 453 9472)* and Christ Church Cathedral *(www.ccdub.ie; 679 8991)*. The sound of their choirs letting loose on Mozart's 'Missa Brevis in D' or Brahms' 'How Lovely are thy Dwellings Fair' really is a most uplifting and transcendental experience. Most days at matins and evensong you can stroll in, grab a pew, and be lifted by a wave of harmony. Programmes are seasonal and attending at Christmas for example is a uniquely local way to mark the passing of the year.

The lead-up to Christmas brings us into 'town' in droves come **December**. The hawkers adopt seasonal themes, the voices of Grafton St's young carol singers fill the place with festive atmosphere, and Christmas trees are bought, sold and dragged along Camden St. Finally, grin and bear the ching-ching of consuming and the awful shopping muzak that drives us all back to drink; and then clink glasses, sing a bit more, and start again.

A SING-SONG AT CHRIST CHURCH

Searching for Silence

"Personally I have no bone to pick with graveyards, I take the air there willingly, perhaps more willingly than elsewhere, when take the air I must." **Samuel Beckett**

Turning into Mount Jerome Cemetery in Harold's Cross, the rumble and screech of traffic plays out behind me. It's the middle of the morning, no one has died, so what am I doing in a cemetery? Just searching for a little bit of peace and quiet.

And within 20 paces, 'noise' disappears. It's a bit disconcerting really, how quickly it fades. The romantic in me imagines there's some kind of natural reverence obeyed even by traffic. But more likely it's a solemn sound barrier provided by a stretch of big old tombs. Absorbing the silence, I am suddenly calmer.

The slatey gravel of the path crunches underfoot. The closely packed tombstones are in various states of repair. Many of the names are of old soldiers, or young soldiers long dead, and I have my own Willie McBride moment. Mount Jerome was the Southside's main Protestant graveyard and its silence and emptiness reflect Dublin's faded Anglican tradition. Many of these graves belong to forgotten families. Who visits them now? And must Protestant cemeteries be quieter places? There is nothing sad or morbid about the quiet; it feels calm and reflective.

I sit on the edge of a crumbling tomb, close my eyes, and try to detect the quietest thing I can hear. I can hear the traffic, yes, but blended together now into a soft hum; fainter again are church bells in single long tolls, slightly sad, perhaps from the reflective sense of mortality in the graveyard. A dog barks, the distance taking the sharpness from his yelp; I hear a bird, no, *two* birds, one calls and the other answers in a twirling, whistling lilt – magpies, I reckon. There's the rhythmic ring of a hammer on metal far, far off, a rough construction noise transformed by distance into a harmonious reply to the church bells.

I savour the aural space and appreciate subtle sounds not *demanding* attention. A woman laughs, some way off, it could even be on the Northside I'm thinking. She doesn't have a care in the world; the lightness of her laugh flutters like a feather in the wind and makes me smile. Deeper, deeper still, I find the quietest noise is the sound of my own breath, slow, regular and easy. Later in town, I 'see' loud noises, like roadworks and the scream of a saw cutting through brick. I glide past them, almost fortified by the silence of that morning. Joyce said, "an Irishman needs three things, silence, cunning and exile," and I think I understand a little of what he meant.

We talk a lot, we joke a lot; but quiet time, slow time, time apart to reflect, is every bit as encoded in a Dubliner's DNA as the need for good company and a laugh. In fact, do the two not go together? Perhaps it's the quiet, contemplative moments that charge our batteries, warm the deeper recesses of our hearts, allow us to know and like ourselves a little better, and let us be light and fun in the company of others.

WHAT IS THE QUIETEST THING
YOU CAN HEAR RIGHT NOW?

Academy
Nº 1
LONDON
MADE
MARK

Staged Sounds

Music courses through the veins of our fair city, with a joyful fusion of rock and roots cascading down the years. It's all around us, from social sing-alongs to stadium concerts and midnight queues outside HMV. But from a slow perspective, we nominate the passionate busker that catches you unawares, the traditional session that connects us with the centuries, and classical interludes that transcend the ordinary and touch the sublime.

TRADITIONAL MUSIC

In rushing towards the cosmopolitan, Dubliners had an ambivalent relationship with traditional music, a genre often regarded as the preserve of tourists and rural folk with nicotine-coloured fingers and beer-stained beards. But in more recent years, feeling thoroughly modern, we re-embraced that most evocative vein of traditional expression. Traditional Irish music was in the doldrums during the 20th century and immigrants are owed a debt for helping to keep it alive. In fact, it was they who came up with the 'traditional' session and brought us back a most enjoyable and convivial way to connect with our roots.

A session at the intimate shack that is the **Cobblestone** *(77 North King St; 872 1799)* is a slow and organic process. At 8pm it might be little more than a fiddler and mandolin player plucking away in the corner, half-finishing tunes while they chat and sup. Of course, the essence of a session lies in the spontaneity of not knowing who'll show up. It's fun to watch stray musicians arrive in ones and twos, carrying leather instrument cases of all sizes and shapes, receiving a welcoming nod and smile from those already playing. Patterns emerge; the flautist always seems to be female, the bodhrán player the biggest drinker, and someone on strings takes the lead. Sessions are also modest, not demanding your upright, undivided attention, leaving room for talking and dreaming. They build slowly, but they build, and by the end of the night there could be up to 15 players banging out wild reels and passionate hornpipes, and every hand in the bar seems to be tapping a tabletop or thigh.

The front snug of **Hughes** *(Chancery St; 872 6540)* is the cosiest spot to hear traditional music in the city. You're literally part of the tight musicians' circle and everyone is encouraged (but not forced) to sing a song.

We have a bit of a *grá* for the old-school, tea-and-biscuits approach of **Comhaltas Ceoltóirí Éireann** *(www.comhaltas.ie)*. It has branches all over the city, and there are informal sessions at least one night a week where a rash of dancing usually breaks out. Some of these branches (Lucan, for example) even have 'Slow Adult Sessions' for the more musically challenged among us who are trying to learn an instrument at a pace that suits. The Clé Club in **Liberty Hall** *(www.libertyhall.ie; 889 2640)* on Wednesday nights promotes Dublin folk songs and particularly songs of the labour movement, and it's a great place to practise your ballads for the next wedding or funeral.

GIVE US A BREAK; IT'S THE ONLY CHICHÉD PHOTO IN THE BOOK

CLASSICAL Dublin's classical heritage goes back to and beyond the first performance of Handel's *Messiah* in a Music Hall in Fishamble St. Wrote one newspaper reviewer: "The sublime, the grand, and the tender, adapted to the most elevated, majestic and moving words, conspired to transport and charm the ravished heart and ear." Classical was still big in Joyce's day (and Joyce himself was said to be quite the tenor) but the pomp and circumstance didn't fit with 20th-century Dublin and classical faded like ink on an old score.

But there are some great little venues from which to tune into the cascading tinkle of the piano and the swelling hum of a cello. The Sunday at Noon concerts at the neoclassical **Hugh Lane Gallery** *(Parnell Square; www.hughlane.ie; 222 5550)* have been running since 1976 but few seem to know just how magically relaxing they are. **Farmleigh House** *(Phoenix Park; www.farmleigh.ie; 815 5990)* hosts a series of summer salon concerts in the lovely small ballroom, and Ballet Ireland performs outdoors on the front lawn.

BUSKING We have a special fondness for the DIY merchants that pop up all over the city, perhaps clocking them as the next Glen Hansard or Damien Rice. Unexpected melodies can clear our heads, and the best buskers raise moods as well as smiles.

The cashed-up Southside attracts most of the roving musicians, with Grafton St particularly prime real estate. We prefer the less hurried atmosphere and superior acoustics of adjacent **Johnson Court**, where an older lady with a squeezebox often leads a merry band of rag-tag music makers. **Merchant's Arch** and the tunnel leading to **Meeting House Square** are both shaped to give shelter and a sonic boost to the plaintive, guitar-slinging singer-songwriters lamenting lost love and opportunity.

Voices of Dublin

While television bombards us, radio keeps us company. We're often more familiar with the tones of our favourite presenters than we are our friends.

The soft, slow articulations of unflappable muso John Kelly on Lyric FM sound like drivetime sanity when all the other stations are trying sell something. For 50 years, the hippity-hop jauntiness of Kerryman Micháel Ó'Muircheartaigh's poetic GAA commentaries have been the soundtrack to summer; he's been described as "one part commentator to two parts *seanchaí*". And the voice of Ronnie Drew was so gravelly it verged on pantomime, but when he sang, his deep Dub intonation embodied the lament of the vanishing old city and its working class.

Our street traders have perfected the economy of language in their breathless "sparklers-five-for-a-euro" Halloween cries; on-course bookies prefer the melodic "seven-to-two-the-field" tic-tac yodels; while newspapers vendors never recovered from the demise of the *Evening Press*, their rhythmic "*Herald* or *Press*!" shortened to the rather forlorn "*Even'Herald*".

smell

SCENTS AND LOCAL SENSIBILITY

> "YOU'RE ONLY HERE FOR A SHORT VISIT. DON'T HURRY, DON'T WORRY. AND BE SURE TO SMELL THE FLOWERS ALONG THE WAY."
>
> Walter Hagen

What, a chapter about smelling Dublin?! Is that a whiff of incredulity we can detect? But don't turn your nose up at the idea right away. There is no other sense as instinctive, emotive or imaginative as smell.

It has a long but selective memory, so the hint of a familiar scent can cast us back to childhood summers, succour us in times of stress and make us feel positively intoxicated. A scent can hit without warning, clearing our mind of everything else. An elusive smell can pleasantly haunt us all day as we try to locate it in time and place. It's no wonder retailers are scrambling to develop scent marketing to captivate passive customers.

So there, smell might make a good slow guide to inspire us to re-explore our hometown after all. As newborns recognise their mothers by smell, perhaps Dubliners too get an innate sense of belonging from familiar scents, flavours that lie so deep in our subconscious we're not even aware of them until they're removed. We live in an old city and time has rewarded it with a wide bouquet of signature scents; some can be savoured year-round while others – like the trace of sandalwood incense during holy week – are fleeting, instinctively tying us to time and place.

The Eau Almanac

As the faint pong of the fireworks fades on 1 January, collectively we hold our noses in the air and contemplate the year ahead. The winter air freshens and cleanses, creating a blank canvas for us to start gathering a *scents* of season. What does **January** in Dublin smell like to you? Is it the musky smoke hanging in the air from briquette fires? The sharp wintergreen sting of football dressing rooms, or the metaphorical trace of bullshit as New Year's resolutions come undone?

The smell of a burger that's just hit the griddle drifting out of the side vents of Rick's on Dame St warms us up on a blustery **February** day. Winter rains in February help to bring out an olfactory symphony: the damp leather perfume of boots and shoes drying in the corner, the remote earthy trace of new mud on the playing fields of Bushy Park, and the welcome no-smell neutrality of the Liffey when it's full. Cozy Simon's Place in the George's Street Arcade is ideal on a bitter day and their top smells are warm, homemade cimamon rolls in the afternoon and hot, strong coffee all day.

We can't avoid the aroma of newly cut daffs when **March's** Daffodil Day charity frenzy ensures every second buttonhole has a fresh flower attached. The mucky but subtle bouquet of shamrock is fading from modern Paddy's Day, replaced by the sulphur of late evening fireworks, the fresh paint of finished-that-morning parade floats and the trace of booze on every young man's breath.

Pluck a new leaf from a city tree – a native ash does the job – crush it in your hand, raise it to our nose and inhale. Each variety has a different smell, but they are usually minty, sharp or oily, an evolutionary trick to discourage animals from snacking on them.

With Easter usually falling in **April**, it smells like the nutmeg tang of hot cross buns, fresh cocoa of thin chocolate Easter eggs, and the lingering sandalwood incense and extinguished candles as the masses of holy week stack up. Fish shops are at their Good Friday busiest and stinkiest before the big day and there's always something fishy about politicians and businessmen schmoozing and boozing together at the Fairyhouse Easter Racing Festival. In the mountains a carpet of bluebells fills the air with its delicate scent, half-hiding the sweat of unfit hikers and cyclists grunting through the first outing of the year.

First communions on **May** Saturdays reek wonderfully of badly applied shoe polish, crumpled old euro notes and hairspray wildly applied to reluctant eight year olds. A trip to Wicklow when the gardens of Mount Usher are hitting their blooming best is a guaranteed reward of competing natural fragrances; rhododendrons, purple and white crocuses and the first brash magnolias.

Rose gardens come into their own in **June**, with the almost artificially perfect scent filling these crimson red corners of the Iveagh Gardens, St Anne's Park and Ardgillan Castle in Balbriggan. The parks and public gardens are also ripe with the familiar, evocative scent of fresh-cut grass, connecting us instinctively with carefree childhood summers.

In **July**, the jasmine in the Chester Beatty Library gardens wafts over the lunching office workers – just about outmuscling the pong of their stinky tuna and sweating salami sandwiches – and hits you hard with a hint of the exotic a full 30 yards away. This is the busiest month for the Temple Bar Market with its pungent essence of smoked oysters, Irish blue cheeses and organic spicy hotdogs. The still-dusty carrots and early spuds have a sandy soil smell and the buttery pastry of the cake stalls adds a little sweet savour.

Bagatelle must have written the accidental slow anthem 'Summer in Dublin' in July because, although nowhere near as bad as in its malodorous heyday, the 'Sniffey Liffey' can still stink like hell at low tide on a hot day, with an oily stench wafting over the quays (and the 46A can still smother your humming).

The inner-city horse owners of the Smithfield market make the warm agricultural whiff of horsepoo a year-round constant, a brash hint of country in the middle of the concrete jungle. But in **August** the Horse Show at the RDS takes the scent of manure to a whole new level. Throw in the saddle soap, the warm leather, the fresh straw and the expensive colognes of the well-heeled, and you have a nose-feast fit for the lord mayor.

African immigrants have increased the number of outdoor barbeques in the Phoenix Park exponentially and their meaty smoke drifts in your windows as you drive through on a busy August Sunday. Try out your nearest public tennis courts for that quintessential summer smell of a sudden shower on dusty, warm tarmac. Parnell St bustles in summer, with Chinese families hanging out outside

Common Scents

- Stop and smell the flowers, crush herbs and even leaves in your hand and breathe in the scent. You might not always smell something, but when you do it will put a spring in your step.
- Examine the contents of your fruit bowl. Feel the skin, study the form, smell the goodness.
- Go to your favourite bakery and just breathe.
- Immerse yourself in the smell at the crook of your partner's neck. If you're lovestruck, take a piece of his/her clothing with you, so you can inhale them at will.
- Create a sanctuary in your home by burning your favourite oils and aromatic candles. Sprinkle a few drops of citrus oil on the floor of the shower, out of the water, and let the steam bring it alive. Make your own air freshener by mixing a few drops of a relaxing essential oil – like lavender or chamomile – with water in a spray bottle.

the string of new restaurants emitting the mouth-watering aromas of lemongrass, hoisin sauce, lime and sizzling fish.

Hot days in **September** are the last chance – for the sensible among us at least (see Lunacy in the Play chapter) – to take a dip and late-summer baptism in seaweed and salty water. Better again is the lingering smell of the brine on your skin for the rest of the day, an enduring reminder that you're alive and making the most of it.

For some reason horseracing fans seem to love pipes and cigars, and their thick aromas hang heavy in the buzzing betting ring at the Leopardstown Races on Champion Stakes Day. The sappy fragrance of a new hurl belongs to All-Ireland Sunday along with the sweet fried onions of a hundred burger vans on the roads out of Croker.

The return of the students and what's left of the warm weather ensure the quintessential smell of the Dublin bus is ramped up to the max (and there's a sharp spike in the strength of the clean chemical smell as you pass the American laundrette on George's St).

Our most arresting autumn scents are in the damp, woody smells of fungi growing on the roots of native trees in Dublin mountain woodlands and St Anne's Park. The species' scents vary from the subtle bark-like smell of the common mushroom to what biologist Éanna Ní Lamhna calls the "blocked sewer" of the stinkhorn. Transferred to a buttered frying pan, mushrooms transform their bouquet to something altogether more meaty and succulent.

As the weather begins to chill in **October**, we really appreciate tree-lined streets that are alive with the seasonal fragrance of wet leaves and the woody hint of damp bark, and an October storm brings the briny trace of the sea all the way up the Liffey. The month ends with Halloween when the cloying smell of toffee apples competes with the wonderfully nutty whiff of Brazil, monkey, almond and hazel nuts in every greengrocer. The nostalgic smell of bangers hangs in the air long after the bang has banged and the kids have run away, and a pleasant trail of burning wood laced with a hint of tyre rubber drifts high across the city and suburbs from the bonfires.

The good-bad smell of late season hiker's socks drying on the fire at the Blue Light pub is a decent herald of **November**. We head indoors to the Savoy with the lightly burned scent of its popcorn machine and the uniquely cinematic aroma of old velvet seats and hastily cleaned floors. Cafes smell of strong tea, fatty rashers just off the pan and wet umbrellas in the corner. A low tide at Sandymount allows the almost overpowering, sea-rich flavours of the mudflats to drift inland, and cycling past nearby Roly's Bistro you might catch the mouth-watering morning waft of vegetable stock being boiled up for the cold day to come.

We all have our own favourite scents of **December's** run-up to Christmas. Close up, the giant tree in O'Connell St is a pine-fresh hint of a distant Norwegian wood, but the delicious yet slightly sock-like aroma of brussels sprouts is an equally quintessential festive aroma. Does Christmas wrapping have a smell? Or are we just dreaming up a slightly inky scent that stays on our hands long after we've opened our presents? A walk along the shore in the last few days of the year always seems to catch the sea air at its freshest and most brackish, the perfect seasonal hangover cure. Or is that a dream too?

Ode to the Smell that Lingers

Dublin memories are filled with fragrances of factories now closed, like Boland's Mills at Grand Canal Dock, Rowntree Chocolates Factory in Kilmainham, John Player ciggies on the South Circular, Jameson Distillery in Smithfield and Jacob's Biscuits on Bishop St. These smells all felt intrinsic to Dublin and now they're all gone. Which is partly why we so unashamedly celebrate a scent that has infused our city for more than 250 years…Guinness.

It's 48 paces from the front door of Ryan's *(117 James's St; 679 0528)* to St James's Gate, which makes it the closest pub to the Guinness brewery. I paced it out. I live in the Tenters, about 600 metres as the seagull flies from St James's Gate. If the wind is blowing from any sort of southerly direction I can sometimes catch a vague whiff of the brewery from my front garden. There are two distinct smells. The first is a strong and harsh yeasty odour that my girlfriend turns her nose up at but I find bracing and challenging, like a good cheese. The other, rarer and fainter, is a much mellower, rich roasted-coffee fragrance with a hint of warm bread about it. It smells like pure pleasure.

Both smells have always charmed me, partly because I know they have hung over my house and the whole neighbourhood for hundreds of years. With the Sniffey Liffey now mostly cleaned up, surely this beautiful beery whiff is Dublin's defining smell? At a more basic gut level, the smell of Guinness makes me want to have a pint. So, a while back, when the wickedly seductive scent struck (the sweeter variety), I decided on a whim to drink a pint in the closest place to the source. The closer I got the stronger the smell grew until I hit James's St and it came on thick and pungent and I could feel it tickling the back of my throat. So I found Ryan's.

For a lot of foreign visitors the Guinness harp is the official symbol of Ireland and they flock in massive numbers to the Guinness Storehouse, the company's museum. For me the high-tech, noisy, gleaming glass and chrome Storehouse captures very little of the simple magic of stout. It feels more like a shrine to the brand than to the pint; a temple to the advertisers rather than the master brewers; to the marketing men, not the barrel rollers. It is brash, cold, hurried and slick, everything a good pint is not. No, if you want to pay homage to our favourite black and white drink then head to Ryan's, a place I soon learned to be honestly and intimately connected to the history and mysteries of Guinness.

The post-box green, old-school bar looked small from the outside and was even tinier once through the front door. It was a lazy afternoon and the place felt quite full, even though I counted only 12 punters. They were all men, mostly locals it seemed, and I heard murmurs about jockeys and horses. The Guinness smell was a little fainter than out on the street, but it still permeated every corner of the little room. I ordered a pint and sat down on my own. The glass was cool but not cold. I raised it to my nose and sniffed. For me the smell of stout is not easy or childish, it is a slightly bitter, mature aroma that will never become old. It is an acquired pong that keeps on giving. I recognised it as a little cousin of the larger smell that filled the whole bar and the streets beyond.

Two older men at the table beside me spotted what I was up to and smiled. I think they thought I was a tourist (I suppose I was, on an olfactory outing). "It's the roasted barley," said one. "That's what you're smelling." I asked him if it was the same thing that caused the smell outside on the street. "What smell?" He looked incredulous. I motioned towards St James's Gate, "The brewery?" They both laughed and told me that they had lived in the Liberties so long that they didn't notice it anymore, it had faded into the background of their everyday. They explained to me that the harsher of the two brewery smells was the hops being boiled, while the sweeter scent was when they put the barley in the roasting house.

I noticed how they drank their pints, tiny in their big hands, gone in three or four big gulps with long gaps between; room for talking. Finishing each other's sentences, these local historians proceeded to tell me the story of Ryan's. I learned that on this very spot stood the first pub to sell Guinness. In the mid-18th century, not long after the brewery opened in 1759, this corner was a gathering point for locals who took casual work guarding the barley that arrived from surrounding farms for the Guinness factory (they still use local barley today). So some bright spark recognised an opportunity and opened a little tavern. I looked around the bar and caught a glimpse of the peasants, covered in golden barley dust from their days work on the wagons, savouring a pint of the final product. It was harder to imagine Guinness ever being something new in Dublin, so integral has it become to the city's life, like the river and the sea.

In Ryan's today, the old drink is everywhere to be seen. Every customer is drinking it, the bar mats are sponsored by it and the old posters on the wall announce it as "a valuable natural aid in case of insomnia." But unlike the Storehouse and the tourist traps of Temple Bar, these posters have been on the walls since they were printed in the 1920s. Guinness is not so much a brand here, as an elixir of the workingman. The more you try to package and promote a tradition, the more it eludes you. Ryan's reeks of it.

Time for another gulp. Roasted barley. Yes. I inhaled deeply and let the subtle, chocolatey vapour fill my nostrils and drift down into my mouth. I rolled a mouthful around my tongue, relishing the contradiction of tart and honeyed tastes. And I felt connected to all the Dubliners who've drank in this room over the centuries, bound by the sensory delight of a pint of Guinness in Ryan's.

Anto Howard

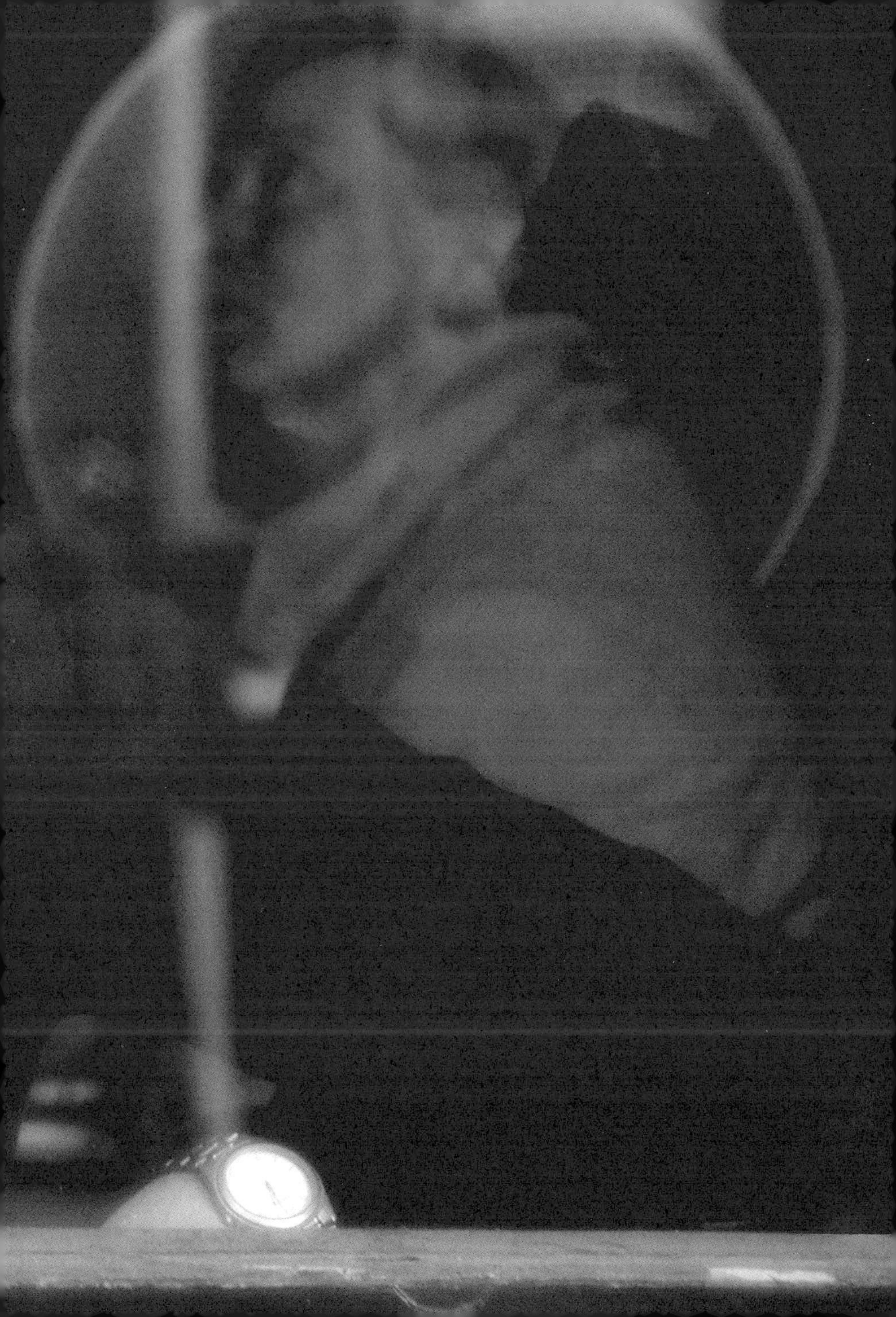

taste

CHARACTERISTIC FLAVOURS

> " **GIVE ME THE SPOTS ON THE APPLES**
> **BUT LEAVE ME THE BIRDS AND BEES.** "
>
> Joni Mitchell

Wouldn't life be unbearably bland without taste, perhaps the most important sense through which we enjoy the world? Eating is one of the few things that involves all the senses and that we can do together, so we really should make the most of Dublin's handsome bounty.

But first, to Rome. In 1986, when a McDonald's was slated to open beside the Spanish Steps, Italian food writer Carlo Petrini decided (no doubt after plenty of yelling, crying, beseeching God and waving his arms around) that the culture of fast food had encroached too far. The mass production, uniformity and blandness of international chains and supermarkets were too much for this passionate Italian to bear and so, brandishing bowls of penne, he led a protest against mass production.

He was one of the first to put a positive spin on the word 'slow' and lit spotfires of creative dissent around the world, prompting people to re-engage with food and consider the cost of the convenience we had so enthusiastically embraced. The principles of this movement have percolated through society, and we as a community have become more mindful of what we do for nourishment. And, far from being puritanical, people who subscribe to these values are dedicated to pleasure – individual, collective, sustainable, natural, traditional and sensory pleasure.

MICHELLE DARMODY OF THE CAKE CAFE

A Whisk in Time

"Slow food is not a gastronomic event where people sit about drinking expensive wine and eating hand-made chocolate," explains the passionate, feisty Michelle Darmody of the **Dublin Slow Food Convivium** *(www.slowfoodireland.com)* and owner of the serenely slow **Cake Cafe** (see page 106). She stresses the grassroots, educational nature of the organisation that arrived here in the mid-90s and now has three thriving city groups (called convivia) in Fingal, Dún Laoghaire/ Wicklow and Dublin proper.

Made up of volunteers drawn from all walks of life, the Slow Food folk organise farmers' markets, festivals, food and wine tastings, mushroom hunts, seaweed gathers, cookery classes, workshops, dinners and trips to organic farms. So strong is the movement here that in 2008 Ireland hosted the international Terra Madre Slow Food festival.

Michelle's particular *grá* is for Irish apples in all their flavours, shapes and smells. This humble fruit is a great ambassador for Irish slow food, or at least it would be if you could find local varieties. "Dublin supermarkets only stock uniform, bland, imported varieties like Granny Smiths, and that's all people know," says Michelle, "when we could be enjoying the delights of our infinitely superior Widow's Friend or a Kerry Pippin." Slow Food is working with small orchards and farmers' markets to preserve the grand tradition of apple-growing in Ireland until, it seems, the rest of us catch up. An apple, Michelle says, can be a fast or slow food. Bought by the roadside from a local orchard in autumn, it's quintessentially slow; plucked from a supermarket shelf in spring, after it was picked early, ripened with chemicals and shipped on a carbon-spewing plane from South Africa, it's indubitably fast.

Although primarily about pleasure, Slow Food presents many challenging, ethical questions. What price the convenience of the cheap, quick feed? What cruelty was inflicted to produce that rasher or those eggs? How much fossil fuel was required to transport that kiwi fruit? How many tea-pickers were exploited to make your early-morning cuppa? How many chemicals does it take to produce a perfectly formed shiny red pepper? Did I just eat the last cod? It's almost enough to put you off your food, if there wasn't a simple and delicious way to be part of the cure.

Slow Food is succeeding in Ireland because we all respond well to things that are more flavoursome and distinct, as long as they're properly introduced. Michelle is optimistic that people are becoming more mindful of what they eat, and points to the resurgence in traditional Irish cheesemaking as an example. Once close to dying out, names like Desmond Raw and Gubeen are now on the tip of cheese-lovers' tongues, literally and metaphorically. First the markets had them, then the delis and the restaurants, and now even the supermarkets are responding to customer requests for a good Bellingham Blue.

Filling Your Basket

We all appreciate the convenience of supermarkets occasionally, but buying produce from a farmers' market, deli or greengrocer and supporting independent local businesses is infinitely more rewarding. It's more fun when you know who you're buying from, particularly if they are characters like old-school grocer Jack Roche (see page 99) and passionate organic butcher Derrick Boulger (see page 101). Dublin has great 'food streets' where you can stroll in the fresh air from small shop to even smaller shop; Meath and Camden are two of the best and both have a couple of classy, chilled-out cafes for refuelling.

Better still is to buy organic. Sure, it costs more to wait patiently for nature to take its course than to artificially hurry the process, but what else do we purchase on price alone? We don't buy the cheapest, crappiest mobile phone, so why nourish ourselves with the cheapest, crappiest meat and veg? Yes, money is tight but factor in the benefits to health, community, environment and flavour, and you might consider organics a bargain. Besides, organics aren't actually that much more expensive when you go to the markets in season; around 20% according to our survey. Are you worth that?

FARMERS' MARKETS

The best thing to happen in Dublin's food scene over the last decade is the growth of farmers' markets countering supermarket-bland and delivering tasty, local, seasonal and often organic produce to mindful Dubliners. They also present rare opportunity to meet the people who produce our food and to chat about what's in season, how to cook and combine different produce, and what home-grown delights have been hidden under your nose. They've also become buzzing community gatherings where neighbours and friends get together and, without even thinking about it, slow down.

Some have glorious natural settings, like the stables courtyard of restored Farmleigh House, the west pier in Howth, and People's Park in Dún Laoghaire. Who doesn't prefer the company of warbling birds or a whispering sea over mind-numbing supermarket muzak?

Many stalls reappear at different markets, but most have a decent quota of smaller, one-off vendors providing a uniquely local flavour. Naturally, the markets vary in quality and value depending on the time of year, and a few hardly deserve the term 'farmer', so here's a rundown of our personal recommendations.

The 25-year-old **Dublin Food Co-op** *(Thur 2pm–8pm, Sat 9.30am–4.30pm; 12 Newmarket; www.dublinfoodcoop.com)* in the Liberties is the most organic and politically conscientious market in town. They encourage you to join (€20) and contribute two hours' work every seven weeks. The aim is to provide "wholesome, nutritious food and ecologically acceptable products to their members", and they even encourage a *cúpla focail* as you shop. It's not at all po-faced; the large indoor space is a hive of community buzz overflowing with goodness. All the veggies are organic and locally grown. One lovely stall sells an eclectic mix of

wildflowers, dusty berries and muddy spuds that look like they were dug up only minutes before. There's a baker, a cheese stall, organic wines and even eco-friendly cleaning products at the dry goods stall. The place is always packed with kids, and baby-changing facilities are a thoughtful touch.

At least Temple Bar got one thing right. Meeting House Square comes alive each Saturday with the hugely popular **Temple Bar Farmers' Market** *(Sat 10am–4.30pm; Meeting House Square; www.temple-bar.ie; 677 2255),* which insists on local producers only. Highlights include the artisan pastry stall, a huge organic produce stall, J&V Rahara Farm meats, and Judith Wolf's wildflowers.

The crowds come for the fresh fish at the sweetly situated 30-stall **Howth Fishermen's and Farmers' Market** *(Sun and bank holidays 10am–5pm; West Pier, Howth Harbour; www.irishfarmersmarkets.ie; 611 5016),* one of the busiest in the country. You can buy fish and seafood fresh from the same hardy lads who pulled it out of the surrounding waters that morning. With a bit of notice they can have a lobster waiting for you on arrival; great for a bit of dinner-party planning when you want to go slow but have to organise quick. Homemade jams, organic fruit and veg, breads, cakes and organic meat are also on offer, and this market is definitely best in spring and summer.

There's a lovely family holiday vibe at the **People's Park Market** *(Sun 11am–4pm; Dún Laoghaire; 087 957 3647)* on the lush grass of Dún Laoghaire's cute little public park. After filling up a bag or two with organic meat and veg, local seafood, Irish fruit, farm cheeses, or even biodegradable nappies and fair-trade clothes, families often grab a few organic burgers or a free-range Thai curry and picnic on the lawn.

Come for the free tasters and you'll end up buying loads at the **Farmleigh Food Market** *(hours vary, see website; Phoenix Park; www.farmleigh.ie; 815 5900)*. The Victorian internal courtyard gives it a small, intimate vibe. The Irish vegetable stall proudly displays the minimal food miles of their cabbages, turnips and Brussels sprouts all the way from Wicklow. Hick's butchers will whip you up an organic hotdog filled with relish, rocket and peppers all bought from other stalls in the market. Don't miss the baker with his homemade sourdough, rye and spelt bread and traditional heavy fruit loaves.

Although **Blackrock Market** *(Main St, Blackrock; www.blackrockmarket.com; 283 3522)* is not a farmers' market, we have to mention the dependable and dapper JJ who turns up most weekends with whatever he's grown in his Dundrum garden – cabbages, spuds, onions, lettuce, all the old reliables lovingly tended to at the back of his house. A gentle but skilful salesman, his spiel is built on the freshness of his produce, most often plucked from the garden that very morn. "Sure you can still see the dew on that."

By late morning he'll have very little left, a train of regular customers (including some celebrities) having cleaned him out. You can't help but be infected by his passion for vegetable gardening, and he is generous with advice and encouragement to wannabe growers. You'll see him there less in winter, when the frost messes with his supply.

Other popular markets include **Dalkey**, **Marlay Park**, **Docklands**, **Clontarf** and **Ballymun**. Find details at www.irishfarmersmarkets.ie and www.irishvillagemarkets.com.

GREENGROCERS Any specialist that adds to the community is good in our book. Just the word 'greengrocer' evokes images of no-frills places, long established and keen to please. And of course, being a real part of the community, they're priceless emporiums of local news and gossip.

The moment a customer asked for celeriac, **Jack Roche** *(26 Meath St)* knew the Liberties had changed. "We got it for him," says Jack. "We'll get anything if you give us a bit of notice." Jack's shed in the middle of Meath St is as much a part of inner-city Dublin shopping as the Moore St stall-handlers. "We're the oldest original shop on the street; three generations of the family have run it and I started working here when I was only small." Freshness is his mantra and he buys everything from the Smithfield Fruit Market early every morning. He stocks some organic fruit for his "younger customers" and, community-minded as he is, keeps his prices affordable. The atmosphere is usually a combination of Sinatra, gentle banter and good stories. **Norton's** *(17 Meath St)*, just up the road, is another venerable greengrocer still doing everything right.

Denis Healy doesn't have a shop per se, but his organic fruit and veg sells at just about every farmers' market so he's probably your local greengrocer at least once a week. He and his brother run a 100-acre organic farm just outside Dublin. "We have five different types of Irish apples. The less-known, rarer stuff," he boasts with a broad grin. The firm, tart Jonagold is his personal favourite. When he does import produce, he has a special arrangement with a local farmer who exports organic beef. "He sends out his meat and the trucks come back with our fruit and veg. The emissions are halved."

Home Plate

You'll miss the wink and grin of a stallholder, but if you think shopping is taking up too much of your valuable leisure time, which you'd rather spend pottering in the garden or pondering on a cloud, we have two reliable outfits that will deliver organic produce to your door.

Sarah Merrigan of Home Organics *(www.homeorganics.ie; 406 0034)* says most of her customers get a weekly selection of staples, plus a splash of whatever's in season. As much of the selection as possible comes from no further than Wicklow. They lob in some choice recipes and also stock eco-cleaning products.

Owner John Healy of Absolutely Organic *(www.absolutelyorganic.ie; 460 0467)* has been spruiking organics for over a decade and also sources as much local produce as possible. You can pick from a range of organic breads, wines, lamb, chicken, jams and pastas, as well as fruit and veg. John reckons his "customers never need step inside a supermarket again".

BUTCHERS Organic meat is free of antibiotics and growth hormones, and comes from well-kept animals that eat natural feed (produced without pesticides). Healthy animals make healthy humans. It's more expensive for sure, but what you lose in your pocket you make up for in taste, wholesomeness and peace of mind. Perhaps we should be aiming to eat better meat, less often.

Certified organic meat is still a little rare (excuse the pun) in Dublin, but we list the best places to find it. We've also included some good traditional butchers who, while not totally organic, do have solid buy-Irish and transparent sourcing policies.

An organic butcher's in Rialto? His friends thought Derrick Boulger was losing it when he opened **Ennis Butcher** *(463 South Circular Rd, Rialto; 454 9282)* in 2005, but word has gone around about this fabulous contemporary butcher dedicated to sustainable and sensitive farming. Real steak-lovers line up to buy his speciality, aged organic beef, hung for 28 days. All his meat is Irish. Derrick shakes his head at the mention of famed Wagyu beef: "It's crap. It's flown in from Japan and all the taste is gone by the time it gets here." He also sells organic lamb, free-range chicken, organic salmon, dairy products and even a few boutique, meat-friendly wines.

The first butcher in the country to go completely organic, **John Downey and Son** *(97 Terenure Rd East; 490 9239)* was simply reacting to customer demand. John himself made the decision in 1991, "because of all the meat scares of the time, mad cows and all that. People wanted organic meat, especially young mothers." Downey's beef (the spiced version is a real treat for the palate), pork and lamb are all top quality, but they've made a name for themselves by expanding into sustainable wild game including boar, venison, snipe, pheasant and wood pigeon.

Eamon Peakin, owner and master butcher of traditional family butchers **Peakin's** *(112 South Circular Rd; 453 5782)*, stocks only organic beef. His grandfather and father worked in the shop when it was owned by the Eastman family, before buying it off them. Eamon is proud of his traditional methods; while a lot of modern butchers and supermarkets buy vacuum-packed meat, he still gets the whole carcass and hangs it for three weeks. "Then I bone it myself," he says. "I like buying the whole animal so I know where it's from, its history." All his other meats are also Irish.

Meath St and Thomas St have a number of free-range traditional Dublin butchers including **Larkin's** *(15 Meath St; 454 2803)* who sell beef and lamb from their own farm, and 100-year-old **Morrissey's** *(12 Wexford St; 465 5467)* which also sells locally caught fish. **Hick's** *(60 Lower George's St, Dún Laoghaire; 280 1433)* have been Wicklow-farmed pork and hand-made sausage specialists since 1927, and you'll see them at many farmers' markets.

BAKERS For such a bread-crazy nation, we chow down on some awfully bland, limp, plastic-wrapped rubbish. No business has suffered more from our enslavement to one-stop shopping than small bakers, and the satisfying crunch, unique shape, rough feel and rich taste of artisan bread are sensual pleasures to seek out and savour. The bakers that have survived are worth crossing suburbs for.

You might have spotted one of their stalls at a farmers' market, but **Soul Bakery** *(24 Main St, Ongar Village; www.soulbakery.ie; 861 4913)* also has a tiny retail space next to their bakery in the Northside suburbs. Proprietor Laurence Kiely comes from a Meath family of bakers and says it's in his blood to be always dreaming up new recipes. All their stock is preservative free and he dismisses the concept of pre-mixed breadmaking. "We take our time and the traditional baking process is a long one, from 10pm till 6am every night." Their range includes Dublin soda breads, fruit breads, seed breads and a host of sticky cakes.

There's nothing fancy or 'artisan' about 40-year-old **Liberty Bakers** *(17 and 42 Meath St)*, but the melt-in-your-mouth, buttermilk taste of a warm loaf of brown bread is their speciality. Everything is baked on premises and the little windows are full of old Dublin favourites like thick-crusted batch loaf and deliciously dense gurr cake, itself a great traditional example of slow. It was devised by Dublin bakers over a century ago, as a way of re-using stale bread and leftover cakes. Because it was so cheap, the cake became popular with children 'on the gurr', gallivanting around town when they were supposed to be in class. The eating of gurr cake became synonymous with working-class Dublin and these street urchins in particular, from whom we got the very Dublin term 'gurrier'.

Bretzel *(1a Lennox St; 475 2724)* has been filling the street with its delicious scent since 1870, and though current owner William Despard isn't Jewish he has preserved the authentic kosher-style of bread making – an echo of a once thriving Jewish neighbourhood around the South Circular Rd. Free of preservatives and treating agents, their bagels and breads taste rich and earthy.

We're blessed with a few great bakery-cafes, a combination that brings together two mediums for community and socially conscious food. Vegetarian, family-run **Blazing Salads** *(42 Drury St; 671 9552)* is really a high-end deli-cafe, but we love them for their choice selection of sourdoughs that includes country white, spelt, multigrain and rye. They use certified organic flours and scorn all artificial improvers, bleaches or, well, anything nasty. Every loaf is shaped by hand and even their salt comes from the local sea.

Tiny, six-stool **Panem** *(21 Lower Ormond Quay; 872 8510)* on the Northside has a more relaxed Italian-cafe vibe (might have something to do with one of the owners being Italian). Everything is baked on site and organic flour is used in all their handmade biscuits, focaccia breads, brioches and traditional fruit breads.

Nary a preservative or additive touches the traditional-style breads of master-baker Owen Doorly at **Il Valentino** (5 Gallery Quay; 633 1100). Thick-crusted Tuscan loaves call out for just a slather of butter but it's the tarts and pastries that are really worth queuing for.

A final mention goes to the ugly midget **kiosk** on O'Connell St near the Savoy cinema that for years now has somehow found the space to bake and serve up the most toothsome doughnuts known to humankind. The choice is simple, iced-chocolate or sugar-coated, and they're so dainty you could down three without blinking, but they really are a multi-sensory delight to be savoured with their still-warm feel, freshly baked smell and honeyed taste. Sneak them into the flicks on a winter evening.

FISHMONGERS **Wrights of Howth** *(1 West Pier, Howth; www.wrightsofhowth.com; 832 0201)* began smoking wild Irish salmon in 1893 and the fourth generation of the family still fillet the fish by hand, cure it with sea salt and smoke it over oak chippings. Their cute little shop on Howth pier also stocks Irish mussels and oysters, and classic Dublin favourites like ray, haddock and mackerel. Their website has a great look-feel-smell sensory test to judge the freshness of fish before you buy. (Also see the Howth Fishermen's and Farmers' Market on page 98.)

For a serious sensory overload, stand before the overflowing fish counter in **Cavistons** *(58–59 Glasthule Rd, Sandycove; www.cavistons.com; 280 9120)* with its strong sea smells and fleshy colours.

Kish Fish *(40–42 Bow St, Smithfield and a smaller shop on Malahide Rd; www.kishfish.ie; 872 8211)* is another family operation. It is supplied by three Irish ports twice daily, and has an unrivalled reputation for the freshest catch.

Fitzsimmons *(83a Kimmage Road West, Crumlin; 455 4832)* is known for its organic salmon and **O'Neill's** *(34 Meath St)* is an old favourite popular with the fish-on-Friday senior local ladies.

It's worth remembering that over-fishing is a stark threat to some species, as the savage decline in sea salmon in Irish waters attests. It's up to consumers to shape demand about what's taken out of the water and what's left in. The Marine Conservation Society's website *(www.fishonline.org)* provides an instant rating on all fish species based on stock status, fisheries management and environmental impact.

DELIS Dublin's delis have been at the forefront of promoting tasty, organic, healthy foods – often with an emphasis on local producers – and encouraging a lifestyle that celebrates good food, wine and company at home.

The husband and wife team of **Fallon & Byrne** *(11–17 Exchequer St; www.fallonandbyrne.com; 472 1010)* have really put it up to the supermarkets in the city centre. You can shop for a whole slow meal here with organic fruit, veg, meat and dairy products on offer, and even a wine cellar downstairs. They showcase seasonal local produce, from Wicklow carrots to handmade chocolates from West Cork.

That the whole shop doubles as a fridge illustrates **Sheridan's** *(11 South Anne St; 679 3143)* dedication to Irish cheeses, which you can sample on a veritable gastronomic tour of the island before you buy. Look out for lesser-known wonders like Cratloe Hills sheep's cheese. Sheridan's specialises in non-pasteurised varieties that use traditional methods to separate the milk, and have been at the forefront of the renaissance in farmhouse cheeses.

Through the farmers' markets where he has a regular olive stall, Brendan O'Mahony stocks his **Lilliput Stores** *(5 Rosemeath Tce, Arbor Hill; 672 9516)* with the best local artisan fare. Try the Arisoa coffee roasted in Meath, apple juice from North County Dublin, and cheeses from Cavan and Cork.

Other standout delicatessens include **Liston's** *(32 Lower Camden St; 405 4779)*, **Morton's** *(15–17 Dunville Ave, Ranelagh; www.mortons.ie; 497 1254)* and **Little Italy** *(139–140 North King St; www.littleitalyltd.com; 872 5208)*.

FORAGING Nothing tastes quite as good as food we've gone out, sourced and gathered ourselves. Most of us recall the thrill of picking blackberries and mushrooms as kids, or maybe even gathering mussels along the seashore, but foraging seems to be a dying art around Dublin, more's the pity. Spend a day revisiting this cheap, healthy, satisfying way to fill the larder and you won't be disappointed.

Hedgerows are the one-stop-shop of foraging, and although miles of them have been lost to rampant development there are still plenty to choose from. The best ones are thick and lush and can be found on quiet roads. Firstly there's those juicy, lip-staining early-autumn **blackberries**, perfect for a jam or crumble (just don't pick too low down where a walking dog might have marked its territory!). In the same hedge you can pluck a bunch of **elderflowers** on a hot day in early summer – they can be used to make a traditional, tangy, thirst-quenching cordial. **Nettles** are bound to be growing under the hedges and their spring shoots make a pea-coloured, spicy, iron-rich soup, great with a dollop of crème fraîche. The back roads of North County Dublin near Rush and Skerries are good hedgerow spots, as are all the big parks, especially the edges of the Phoenix Park. You'll also find long stretches of them on less busy roads at the foot of the mountains in the south and near the Meath border in the northwest of the city.

Dedicated mycologist Bill O'Dea set up www.mushroomstuff.com to organise his expert-led **mushroom hunts** all over Ireland, with the Wicklow Mountains a favourite foraging ground. Each hunt begins with a briefing from Bill on what to look out for and what to avoid. Ceps, chanterelles, parasols, hedgehogs and chicken of the woods are some of the brilliantly named edible varieties and invariably turn up in the communal lunch made from the morning's harvest. Then it's back out to track down some more native fungi to bring home for tea.

The **Dublin Slow Food convivia** *(www.slowfoodireland.com)* organise similar outings, along with shoreline walks in Dublin Bay to gather **mussels**, **cockles**, **limpets**, **razor shell clams** and **edible seaweeds**.

Wild Garlic is a herb with an extra kick and works well with pasta and soup, and indeed mushrooms. You can find it all over the county in shady woodland areas (a lot of people have it in their gardens) but the Phoenix Park is again a good city spot.

La Vida Locavore

There's an international movement you may have heard about, people known as locavores who, in response to global warming, eat only what's grown within a 100-mile radius of where they live. It's frankly just about impossible, puritanical, and not necessarily all that helpful to the environment. But it's a useful exercise to try for a day. You'll become more conscious of buying local produce, eating seasonally and giving greater thanks for the luxuries we ship in.

MUSHROOM KNIFE

Eating out

Slow Food Dublin doesn't endorse particular places to eat (however much we try to cajole the members to name their favourite spots), but we decided to apply some key slow criteria – natural, local, traditional, sensory, characteristic, most gratifying – to select a few of our favourite options for dining seasoned with a little local flavour.

CAFES

As owner Michelle Darmody is head of Slow Food Dublin, it's no jaw-dropping surprise that her blissful little **Cake Cafe** *(Daintree Building, Pleasants Pl; www.thecakecafe.ie; 478 9394)* is the best place in town to sit down, slow down and chow down on sweet and savoury delights made with a slow hand. Try getting an outdoor seat in the overgrown interior courtyard to soak up the full, laid-back atmosphere.

Local, organic, seasonal produce, biodegradable cleaning products, recycled napkins, ethically sourced coffee roasted in Meath – the place ticks all the right boxes. But it's the traditional tea-shop experience of scrumptious baked goods, dainty mismatched crockery, floral tablecloths and homely service that makes this a little oasis in the city centre.

"We don't have a freezer," boasts Cormac Kenny, owner of **Smock Alley Cafe** *(Smock Alley; 087 648 5390)*. "We make absolutely everything here fresh and totally organic each day." From the bamboo floor (easier to regrow than hardwood) and recycled furniture to the natural paints and low-energy lights, everything here is testimony to Cormac's enthusiastic commitment to sustainability. He's also determined to make the cafe a part of the community and – unlike most eating establishments these days – a place to spend some time: the walls are given over to local artists; parents will enjoy the baby-changing space and ample room for strollers; there are tango classes at the weekend; and a regular guitar player in the corner helps to keep a buzz about the place. The super-simple menu comprises one sensational soup and savoury tart each day, bolstered by a few cakes and sarnies.

It's not very big, but **Bite of Life** *(55 Patrick St; 454 2949)* has been embraced with an open heart by the Liberties community who rely on this classic neighbourhood cafe for spiritual respite. Owner Jorinde Moynihan and her mouthy, fun staff always ensure laughs are on the menu, along with creative sambos and coffee that's loyal to the bean. There's always a loyal congregation of locals and the vibe's as chilled out as St Pat's Cathedral next door.

Occupying a spot in the middle of the Dublin Food Co-op market, **Amnesty International Freedom Cafe** *(12 Newmarket Square)* provides top-notch, organic, ethically sound grub with a side of human rights (man, how much good karma can one place horde?). Their thin-crust pizza is, for our money, the best in the city.

Avoca Cafe *(11–13 Suffolk St; www.avoca.ie; 677 4215)* is the kind of place you and your mammy would love for a sweet after-

noon respite from shopping. They encourage doing things the long way, using natural ingredients to prepare meals from scratch. They are also big supporters of small native food producers like Knockanure oak smoked cheese and Hederman mussels, while organic Irish oatmeal and Hick's smoked back bacon are on the breakfast menu.

Queen of Tarts *(Dame St; 670 7499)* feels like a country tea-shop with serious finesse. The owners are two trained pastry chefs and use only the best ingredients to make their buttermilk soda bread, warm jam tarts and homemade scones, which are all destined to be accompanied by a pot of strong tea. There's plenty of room for prams and mums love it.

We have to mention **Bewley's** *(Grafton St; www.bewleys.com; 672 7720)* of course, the 80-year-old tea-and-bun classic that's synonymous with the word 'cafe' in Dublin. Sitting downstairs in the back, with the light shattered into 20 colours by the Harry Clarke stained glass windows, is still a city-centre pleasure, but since the place became a high-turnover pizza and pasta joint (admittedly a pretty decent one) it's no longer quite so serene or singular.

Black and White Pudding

The surest way to freak out a tourist is to tell them what goes into the black pudding they're scoffing for breakfast. Traditional blood pudding – to give it its real and perhaps less-palatable title – is perhaps one of Ireland's first slow foods. It grew out of the eco-friendly, no-waste peasant notion of using every bit of a precious slaughtered animal. When a pig was killed the intestine was washed and stuffed with onions, spices, cloves, flour, salt, lard and oatmeal, all mixed with the warm blood. The pudding was then poached in hot water.

While mass market puddings are made with dried blood, modern artisan producers like Hugh Maguire *(Ashbourne, Co. Meath; 849 9919)* and PJ Burns *(Sneem, Co. Kerry; 064 45139)* insist fresh blood is essential for that biting aroma and taste. The Maguire pudding has a spicier taste due to a sprinkle of cayenne, nutmeg and pimento. The Burns version is subtler, with pinhead local oatmeal a key ingredient.

In the 'ark' of traditional foods it wants to preserve, Slow Food Ireland have singled out artisan butchers' blood puddings, and restaurants like The Winding Stair (opposite) are doing their bit by incorporating it creatively in several dishes.

Slightly overlooked in the renaissance, but not to be underestimated, white pudding is bloodless and consists of shredded pork and fat, suet, spices, breadcrumbs and oatmeal, again stuffed into a casing. We love it raw – yes, raw – and spread like a pâté on toast. Kelly Butchers *(Newport, Co. Mayo; 98 41149)* is our favourite supplier.

RESTAURANTS Dublin's so-called gastronomic revolution has sometimes been heavy on hype and light on the essentials of quality, time and care. But a bottom-up demand for a bit more soul means there are still plenty of places to delight palate and pocket and not take the whole thing too seriously.

When they took over one of our most beloved second-hand bookshops and hang-out joints, the new owners of **The Winding Stair** *(40 Lower Ormond Quay; www.winding-stair.com; 872 7320)* were smart enough to keep the books downstairs and open a snug gastro-pub restaurant focused on seasonal and artisanal Irish produce on top. Most impressively they've managed to resurrect that much-maligned staple, a traditional collar of bacon with new-season savoy cabbage.

They don't pick up your theatre tickets between courses any more, but an early dinner at **Chapter One** *(18–19 Parnell Square; 873 2266)* and a night at the Abbey or Gate is still one of the most relaxing, indulgent, sensorial ways to spend a long evening in the capital. Owner-chef Ross Lewis is fastidious about the seasonality of his menu and loves to plug all the small Irish food-makers it supports, including Gubeen cheeses and Fingal Ferguson's smoked meats.

A rarity in modern Dublin eateries, the staff at **Gruel** *(67 Dame St; 670 7119)* have mostly worked there for years. It makes for a relaxed atmosphere with lively banter and where-did-you-appear-from quality service. The menu is dictated by whatever produce is at its best at the time, and as a lovely slow touch, chef Nial McGovern tells us that "the baker comes in every morning at 4am and the cakes he makes are completely up to him, it just depends on his mood." We love that, mood cakes.

In a town with no shortage of decent fish and chippers, **The Kingfisher** *(166–168 Parnell St; 872 8732)* stands out for its simplicity and longevity, which is based on incredible value, quality fresh fish and seafood, chips the way we like them and a mixed grill of Irish meats guaranteed to cure a hangover. Fresh spuds and veg come from the owner's own farm.

Becoming synonymous with three-hour dining and wine-fuelled, late-evening craic has kept the **Unicorn** *(12B Merrion Court; 662 4757)* running for more than 60 years. The Italian menu uses produce from the local area and lists where everything comes from, but the sealer for us is that mobile phones are barred. Try to get a spot on the terrace looking out on Merrion Court.

The open, light-filled, ex-warehouse room of **Fallon & Byrnes'** upstairs bistro *(11–17 Exchequer St; www.fallonandbyrne.net; 472 1010)* is our favourite place in the city for an unhurried dinner with friends. "Slow Food, Hot Spot" boasts their slightly naff motto, but the focus is always on locally sourced and often organic ingredients like aged Irish Angus sirloin and Carlingford Lough oysters from their own downstairs deli.

For a spot of al fresco we recommend the communal and continental flair of Quartiere Bloom, the Italian Quarter *(Lower Ormond Quay)*, a buzzing little mix of outdoor dining, music and chatter. If your group can't decide on which place to choose, avoid the stress and just head to **Enoteca delle Langhe** *(Blooms Lane; 888 0834)* and share an antipasto misto and a bottle of wine.

Hail to the Toastie

The pub, of course, is the heart of our social existence. It's the great leveller where status and rank have no meaning, where generation gaps are bridged, inhibitions lowered, tongues loosened, schemes hatched, songs sung, stories told and gossip embroidered. It's a unique local institution: a theatre and a cosy room, a centre stage and a hideaway, a debating chamber and a place for silent contemplation. Above all, it's a tonic for the rigours of reality and the rain. Around the world people have tried to replicate the atmosphere of the traditional Irish pub. They've failed, we've worked out why, and here we reveal the missing ingredient...it's the humble toastie.

It's on a slow, wet afternoon that the pub really comes into its own; a silent temple to slowness, altar to the wasted hour, ashram of wise old geezers. For the perfect slow afternoon, all you need is a good pint of Guinness, the newspaper, and a toasted sandwich, the humblest and most undemanding of boozer's sustenance, which has been the staple of Dublin pubs since the grill was invented. It comes in three choices only: ham and cheese; ham and no cheese; or cheese and no ham. And the only adornment is a lick of mustard or brown sauce. But for some magical, lead-into-gold reason, when eaten in small bites between leisurely mouthfuls of bitter stout before the hour of four, it is transformed into a sensory feast of mouth-melting goodness and nose-tickling aromas.

You probably have your own favourites, but if you're willing to try an old tradition somewhere new, here are three alchemists that get the afternoon toastie just right.

Officially 'The Castle Inn' but known and loved as boozy, late-night gem **Grogan's** *(15 South William St; 677 9320)*, this is an afternoon hideout beyond compare. The old stained-glass panels on the wall reflect back the warm light into the empty, almost-hushed lounge, where the only sounds are the rustle of newspapers and the humming of an idle barman. Owner and host Tommy's collection of bad art on the walls (some of it rumoured to have been handed over in payment of outstanding tabs) is an explosion of rude colour in daylight and always good for a smile.

The sliver of glass, dark wood and red brick that is tiny, ancient **Fallon's** *(129 The Coombe; 454 2801)* is a little off the beaten track, so you're likely to have the place to yourself on a weekday afternoon. If you do feel up for a chat, hopefully the wry, welcoming stalwart Eileen is behind the counter. The place is basically one long window and another quiet spot to ponder the changing light over a slow winter hour.

As long as there's no football game on, you can hear the clip of the barman's leather soles on the ancient tile floor during the afternoon lull in **The Swan** *(Aungier St; 465 2722)*. The odd over-worked, hung-over medical student has been known to nip in for a pint – arguably the best in town – a toastie and a quick snooze in the snug.

WHISKEY If you like the smooth kick of a good Irish whiskey (and if you don't, it's only a matter of time) then **The Celtic Whiskey Shop** *(27–28 Dawson St; www.celticwhiskeyshop.com; 675 9744)* provides a wonderful exploration of the rich history of distilling in Ireland. It was no doubt set up with thirsty tourists in mind, but passionate and knowledgeable staff make it a wonderful spot for locals to savour a tipple that by tradition and lore has been elevated from mere boozing to the essence of the Irish spirit.

The offer of whiskey is on page one of the Irish hospitality manual, a platform for male bonding and an invitation to share the family home. You'd better make sure you've got a decent bottle in the cupboard before you're caught out. After they got together, Irish distillers put all their marketing clout into promoting just a few whiskies, when in fact there are more than 100 brands to choose from. The real pleasure of visiting the Celtic Whiskey Shop is discovering the lesser known tipples like Green Spot and our favourite, Redbreast, which is pure pot still, the way all whiskey used to be made.

But perhaps our favourite slow aspect of whiskey-making is that the final stage cannot be rushed and is supervised by Mother Nature. The clear spirit produced by man can't even be called whiskey until it has matured in casks or barrels for at least three years. It is normally left there for between five and 12 years depending on the whiskey required, during which time some will evaporate. This is known in the industry as 'the angels' share', a phrase probably coined by the first man caught copying keys to the warehouse.

A Pint of Plain

When things go wrong and will not come right,
Though you do the best you can,
When life looks black as the hour of night –
A PINT OF PLAIN IS YOUR ONLY MAN.

In his mental masterpiece *At Swim-Two-Birds*, Flann O'Brien has fictional, working-class Dublin poet Jem Casey pen what has become an oft-recited ode to the miraculous powers of a pint of Guinness, 'The Workman's Friend'.

Of course we all missed the joke; O'Brien, a fierce drinker himself, was trying to send up that very same tendency to romanticise our blind, self-denying, dangerous love affair with the 'auld drop'. All the same, it's hard to recite the poem without falling under the spell of its wink-and-grin refrain.

touch

THINGS THAT FEEL GOOD

“TOO OFTEN WE UNDERESTIMATE THE POWER OF A TOUCH, A SMILE, A KIND WORD, A LISTENING EAR, OR THE SMALLEST ACT OF CARING, ALL OF WHICH HAVE THE POTENTIAL TO TURN A LIFE AROUND.”

Leo Buscaglia

The first sense we develop and the last we lose is touch. It's how we find our place in the world and relate to everything in it. Isn't it strange then that we spend much of our lives with our hands in our pockets, touchy about the whole idea of touch? In the hustle and bustle of the city we can get a little obsessed with personal space. And as a result we become touch-deprived, missing out on a daily reminder of friendship, affection and warmth. Touching and *being* touched can lift our mood, calm anxieties and even strengthen our immune system.

But it's not just the physical aspect of touch that provides benefit – staying in touch socially and reaching out to people can help cure that most modern urban malaise, isolation. Computer screens are dead to the touch and our increasingly virtual world reduces our chances for real human contact.

But don't fret, the solution is in easy reach; just get up from that keyboard and go outside. We can all benefit from greater physical connection with the world around us, whether tactile or emotional, actually feeling something or having our heartstrings pulled. Touching is, after all, the most intimate way of getting to know someone, something or some place.

FEELING THE WEIGHT OF THE WORLD, PORTMARNOCK BEACH

That Dublin Feel

Here are a few ideas to help you really get in touch with your hometown, and experience it as a vital and constantly evolving entity rather than an inanimate frame for your life. Dublin has a history rendered rich in brick and stone, life you can feel in the leaves and bark of its trees, and a potency in the waters of river, sea and rain. As local sculptor Paul Ferriter says, "Dublin feels like rough granite, cold iron railings and the rain on my open hand."

CONSTRUCTED Stone puts things and time into perspective. Let's start with grey Dublin granite, flecked with silver quartz, hard and tough to the touch – a bush-hammered finish they call it in the building trade. You can almost feel the age of it, over 400 million years of patient build-up in the Wicklow Mountains. See, perspective.

Historically, granite was widely available close to the city in places like Three Rock, Kilgobbin and Blessington. Early city fathers favoured it for the facades of our show-off public buildings, like the entrance to Trinity and the GPO as well as made-to-last engineering works like Dún Laoghaire Harbour. Even the ostentatious structures of today, like the IFSC, tap into the gravitas and authority represented by the rock, with granite finishes covering cheaper building materials. A trip to Dalkey Quarry – now beloved by rock climbers – will bring you in contact with granite before it's been polished.

If granite is the show pony of city architecture, then limestone is definitely its workhorse. The rock was more common and cheaper to quarry, and feels sandy and rough under hand. The remaining pieces of the medieval City Wall at Great Ship St and St Audoen's are built of local, muddy grey Calp Limestone, which was quarried from where Donnybrook Bus Station now stands. The spectacular, faultlessly even Customs House is actually made of humble pale limestone, covered in sleek Portland stone to keep up appearances.

You would know you were on a Georgian street by touch alone, specifically the smooth but irregular feel of imperfect Georgian bricks, the not-quite-perfectly-flat feel of the old window glass, and the cool rattle of the black iron railings under your passing fingers. North Great George's St is a good spot to experiment. Ditto for Victorian terraced streets where the polished evenness of the industrial dark red brick contrasts with the jagged roughness of the mortar. The architects of the Golden Age loved their ornamentation, and the likes of James Gandon introduced artificial stone to Dublin. Notice the slightly fake, ceramic feel to the Rutland Fountain opposite the National Gallery and the frieze on the Rotunda Hospital.

At least once in your life, preferably in summer, treat yourself to some DIY reflexology by walking barefoot across some warm, sleek city cobblestones (limestone clasts) in Temple Bar, Trinity or anywhere you can find them. Most of these were collected from nearby beaches, already rounded and polished by millions upon millions of waves, and although many have been re-laid some original cobbles remain from the 19th century. Another tactile treat in the city is running your hand over the assorted coloured rocks that make up the Oscar Wilde statue; itself perched on a granite boulder in Merrion Square.

If it's lucky to touch wood, then our churches and pubs are blessed indeed. A smooth, finished feel dominates their insides, from the ancient hardwood polished benches of St Patrick's to the equally sacred long, curved bars of our finer old pubs like the Stag's Head on Dame Lane or Walshes in Stoneybatter. Exposed, exterior woods naturally feel more worn and full of character, like the creaky wooden bridge across Crab Lake Water at Dollymount, coarse under a swimmer's bare feet; or the black painted timber of the canal locks, rough-hewn under your hand as you shuffle across.

Love materials that proudly show their age, rebelling against a growing vanity that even extends to modern buildings. The cool, solid, varied feel of the many ages of bronze can be found throughout the city centre with our favourites being James Joyce on North Earl St and Patrick Kavanagh on his bench by the Grand Canal. Consider also pathos in the crumbling masonry of the older tombs and gravestones at Mount Jerome near Harold's Cross or the Huguenot Cemetery at Merrion Row, fading testament to lives long lost.

For architecture aficionados, Dublin devotees and nosy-parkers in general, the annual **Open House** *(www.architecturefoundation.ie/openhouse)* festival provides an irresistible opportunity to celebrate our built environment, when doors to buildings normally off limits are flung open and yours to explore. For four days in October you're invited to feel your way around your hometown, from the poured concrete modernity of brand new architects' offices to the 1939 cedar-clad detached Meander House in south Dublin and the translucent projecting glazing of the Dublin City Council Labs.

NATURAL Sometimes even fleeting contact with nature is enough to soothe and succour us as we make our way around a modern city. And Dublin provides natural 'feel-good' opportunities aplenty, whether it's running your hand along a hedge, feeling the softness of a magpie feather between your fingers, or kicking through a pile of autumn leaves.

Any chance to kick off shoes and walk on warm grass should be seized with both feet. Different grasses provide different 'soleful' experiences: there's the carpet-soft neatness on the lawns of St Stephen's Green and Merrion Square; the flick and flutter of meadow grass in the Phoenix Park; or the sharp keep-you-on-your-toes brush of marram grass by the sea.

Trees provide opportunity for roaming hands. Leaves are as different in their textures as in their shapes, from the prickly needles of the spruce to the smooth-ribbed wild elm. With your eyes closed you could pluck a leaf from a silver birch on the North Circular Rd and guess the season by how dry or moist it feels as you crush it in your palm. We reckon the most essential slow action would be to spend an afternoon reading this book while sitting under a tree, pressing your back into a perfectly shaped nook of its immovable trunk. Notice the different bark surfaces of various species, comparing a craggy, rugged oak to a sleeker ash.

BEACHCOMBING ON BULL ISLAND

BEACHES AND COVES

The first plunge of the summer is an exhilarating embrace with nature. Whether we're strolling, exploring, playing, basking or just collecting shells, the beach allows us to indulge our sense of touch. And, of course, the *lack* of touch – the comfort of space and open vistas; a place that hasn't been fenced off, become private property or been earmarked for development.

Each Dublin beach takes on the characteristics of its broader neighbourhood and attracts its own loyal frolickers. For Northsiders it's the rolling dunes and big waves of working-class **Dollymount** or 'Dollier', now a favourite haunt of kite and wind surfers along with hordes of wild birds. An ankle-deep tumble through the silky-soft dunes and ankle-whipping grasses is a guaranteed nostalgia-fest.

You have to negotiate a pretty steep climb to get down to the wonderfully secluded, rocky little coves below **Howth Head**, but the solitude is well worth the effort. Sit atop a huge, sturdy boulder and contemplate the rhythm of the waves. For the less sure-footed, the little polished-pebble beach near Howth Village is a kid-friendly option close to a reliable purveyor of ninety-nines.

The Southside – as usual – is spoiled for choice. **Sandymount Strand** has traditionally been the city's favourite beach for strolling and dog walking, its dodgy water quality discouraging of a dip. The flattened sand feels cool underfoot and a wide expanse of shoreline opens up with the retreating tide. At low ebb of an evening, walk out to the sea's edge and feel the chilled water between your toes as the stars come out and the lighted ships sneak past in the bay.

Pretty as a picture with a Martello Tower as a backdrop, the **Forty Foot** is our iconic, deep swimming hole and has a convivial all-inclusive atmosphere. The camaraderie reaches its peak in winter when the temperatures drop (see the essay on page 156), and the cool burn of a nip of whiskey is the traditional tonic for just-out-of-the-water shivers. The little sandy beach just before the Forty Foot is a bucket-and-spade suntrap protected by a tall, solid granite wall that warms up nicely as the day progresses. The chalky surfaces of idyllic cliffside **Vico** and **White Rock** are gentle against the skin and perfect for basking in between languid dives into the fishtank-clear waters.

Stony, sheltered and sublimely cosy, **Killiney Beach** has a gentle gradient that reassures kids and hopeless swimmers alike. It's also a tactile delight, with weird and wonderfully textured shells (with names like Beaded Periwinkle, Van Hyning's Cockle and Imperial Venus) and pebbles (mostly from the glacial cliffs of the beach) always washed up on shore. Killiney Hill beckons for a nature walk and the chance to work up a sweat.

“ ONE TOUCH OF NATURE MAKES THE WHOLE WORLD KIN. ”

William Shakespeare

Mucking In

Isn't it ironic that in a place with so many co-habiting at such close quarters, isolation is perhaps the greatest malaise? The best way to heal urban fractures is to connect with the wider community, the people who live and work around us. Two slow remedies we recommend are community gardening and volunteering.

GARDENS Community gardeners – and all the joy, fun and focus they bring to their local areas (not to mention fresh veggies) – provide inspiration to muck in for the greater good.

Nobody would nominate Clondalkin as particularly green, but Pat Harrington and some local kids have created a little oasis of natural food and wildflowers in the organic community garden of **Colaiste Bhride National School.** Determined to grow fruit and veggies by traditional methods and without chemicals, Pat borrowed a horse and plough from the old ladies who used to own Airfield House and dug the original patch some 20 years ago. A keen letter writer, he gathered support from the wider community, getting equipment donated and even enlisting a bunch of inmates from the nearby prison who helped clear land and build a shed.

But the best workers, he's delighted to point out, have been the schoolkids who have helped him turn their little patch into a bountiful plot of Dublin staples. The students themselves often take home the produce left over after school meals. Other schools like **Gaelscoil Choláiste Mhuire** in Parnell Square and **St Joseph's National School** in Finglas have started similar kitchen gardens that promote healthy eating and help kids appreciate what it takes to get food from dirt to dinner.

The halt of the development boom left some derelict plots, and resourceful community gardeners have been quick to fill the void, turning local eyesores into blooming symbols of civic pride and pleasure. The **South Circular Road Community Food Garden Project** *(corner of South Circular Rd and Rehoboth Pl; southcirculargarden.blogspot.com; 087 734 4904)* has a long name and a succinct mission: to grow organic food.

The group has turned a disused corner of this busy road into a gathering spot for locals of all ages with an interest in growing food the way nature intended. Member William Brennan feels the weakening economy has encouraged more people to seek out the wholesome bounty of the garden. They could hardly be more welcoming, and harvesting and seed-saving time in autumn is a particularly good excuse for a visit.

An inability "to find Irish apples in Tesco in September" was part of the inspiration behind the sustainable, activist and organic **Cursed Earth Garden** *(aka the Phibsboro Community Garden, Royal Canal, opposite Shandon Gardens)*. It too occupies unused land that was "damaged by industrialism". A willow den, compost heap and herb garden are among the garden's delights and the local community quickly took the loosely organised, non-hierarchical affair to their heart. They encourage wannabe members to pop along any weekend, to "walk away from the traffic and dig their hands in dirt". Members often bring some hot food to share.

Pat Dunne and Eileen Kenny have galvanised the local community around their **Greenhills Community Gardens** *(rear of St Peter's Rd and St James's Rd, Greenhills Estate; www.greenhillsresidentsassociation.org; 087 990 2895)*, which has transformed disused land and tapped into that Dublin tradition of allotment gardening.

Dublin Food Growing *(www.dublinfoodgrowing.org)*, promoting "food security from the ground up", is a great local resource to help you start setting up your own community garden. They run workshops and classes and also work closely with the Slow Food folk.

VOLUNTEERING

Advertisers may have diluted the sentiment, but reaching out to touch *is* a life-affirming experience. Volunteering allows us to hook up with like-minded people in the community and gain a lot from giving something back – peace of mind, perspective, even our own self-esteem – and there's no shortage of local organisations who need a hand.

If you're feeling altruistic but don't know where to start, **www.volunteer.ie** is a handy national website developing a network of do-gooding at a local and national level. It has five Volunteer Centres around Dublin, where you can get information on who needs what. You can even register online and wait for the right organisation to get in touch. **Volunteering Ireland** *(www.volunteeringireland.com)* runs a similar service.

The **Dublin Simon Community** *(www.dubsimon.ie)* has been providing relief to Dublin's most impoverished for 40 years now, its soup vans a familiar sight. Volunteer here and you'll quickly be put to work on the streets, working alongside professional staff delivering vital services to the growing number of people experiencing homelessness. You can also be part of their mounting efforts to help people break out of the vicious cycle that leads to homelessness in the first place. Even if you can't volunteer regularly, there are always collection buckets that need rattling, raffle tickets to be sold and other fundraising ideas to be hatched.

Dubliner Dr Thomas Barnardo was born and raised on Dame St, and set up his famous child charity in 1867. **Barnardos Ireland** *(www.barnardos.ie)* encourages volunteers to enter every aspect of the organisation, from working in its local charity shops to help deliver literacy programmes or even being trained as child counsellors.

And if you're gaga about babies, the **Community Mothers' Programme** *(Brenda Molloy, HSE; brenda.molloy@hse.ie; 838 7122)* is a clever voluntary scheme where experienced mothers visit new mums in their area once a month during the first two years of the child's life. The idea is to share learned knowledge in a supportive way so as to empower and reassure new mums.

If nature and conservation are more your cup of herbal tea, **Birdwatch Ireland** *(www.birdwatchireland.ie)* relies on volunteer birders and twitchers for many of its sighting surveys and educational visits, plus a lot of their administration work. And the **Irish Wildlife Trust** *(www.iwt.ie)* runs the hands-on 'Grubby Gang', a volunteer project that encourages Dublin folk to preserve wildlife and habitats in their own communities.

Cultivating Community

Time for an inspirational fairytale about how, like a wildflower poking through a crack in the pavement, a little love and attention helped an entire neighbourhood bloom.

"It all started with the idea of putting a few shared compost bins at the end of the road," says the ebullient Kaethe Burt O'Dea, describing the seeds of the community renaissance in her small corner of Stoneybatter.

"Neighbours met at the compost bins and got talking; basically, people came together through composting," she says, accidentally coining what would be a great environmental logo for our time. Kaethe reckons we all have a "psychologically damaging relationship with waste", and that using the bins made people feel better about themselves.

One thing led to another – in this case, a stinky great mound of life-giving compost that required somewhere to be spread. One inspired local donated a tiny sliver of land at the side of her house and the beautiful little **Sitric Community Composting Garden** *(Sitric Rd, Stoneybatter; compost@desireland.ie; 087 244 4185)* was born.

Interest in the garden grew and, nourished with compost and community spirit, the tiny space was transformed into a blooming gem producing a slew of vegetables, dozens of herbs plus lots of wildflowers, all grown out of locals' leftovers. But what's been created is much more than a bountiful veggie patch.

The community then decided to hold harvest street festivals in June and October, when locals gathered to share and savour homemade dishes made from the garden produce. The all-inclusive spirit encouraged other, non-green-fingered residents to contribute to the community in their own ways. Events now include a clothes swap-fest, music, a sing-song, poetry, face painting and games for kids. Over 200 people are attending these days and Kaethe's only worry is that it might grow too big!

Like-minded souls have been drawn to the area, and people are visiting and being inspired. With the garden established as a focal point, neighbours are constantly coming up with new projects to benefit the area.

They are excited about the idea of 'the lifeline', a brilliantly ambitious plan to turn a nearby disused stretch of the old Great Northern Railway into a large community green space of gardens, walks, woodland and allotments that would have even more far-reaching benefits for everyone. Every new idea, says Kaethe, is about building community and bringing people together.

And it's not just about harnessing nature for their cause; another plan is to create a 'share shop' where, instead of every local buying a new this or that (tools, books, utensils etc), people would share what they've got and reduce the cost of living and consuming for everyone. It's altogether an inspirational glimpse of a utopian world, a tonic for our times, and a shining example of what we can achieve when we pull together.

KAETHE BURT O'DEA AT THE STONEYBATTER PLOT

DO

IN THE PURSUIT OF SLOW

NURTURE

PLAY

MOTION

TRAVEL

SMALL

GATHER

nurture

TAKE CARE OF YOURSELF

“ **NOTHING CAN CURE THE SOUL BUT THE SENSES, JUST AS NOTHING CAN CURE THE SENSES BUT THE SOUL.** ”

Oscar Wilde

Driving all our lives is the search for health and happiness, a simple enough task one would have thought. But we seem to get distracted, whether it's by other people's ambitions, the grind of modern life, the race to get ahead or just a struggle to get by. We become so preoccupied with paving our future, we forget to tread joyfully on the now. Looking out for things that stimulate, satisfy and calm us is as important to our wellbeing as going to the doctor.

It doesn't matter where we seek satisfaction and solace, whether it's in a church, spa, salon, park, cookery class, while collecting orchids, painting nudes, crafting pottery, salvaging furniture or making soap. We just need to take it where and when we can. Don't wait to find the time or you never will. *Make* the time to nurture your mind, body and spirit and you'll find you can accomplish much more, thus magically creating more time.

Mindfulness

Slow the rush of thoughts flooding your brain. Mindfulness is perhaps our greatest gift and the greatest gift we can give back to the planet. Just thinking in the moment about what you're doing will encourage you to get more out of life and feel in control. All you have to do is think about it. You are reading this book. Where are you, in the context of your surroundings? Are you comfortable? What can you hear? Fetch yourself a glass of water. Drink it and say to yourself, "I'm drinking a glass of water". Think about the taste, the purifying goodness.

Think about 'what' you're doing more, instead of 'why' or particularly 'when'. It will help you develop a quiet mind, the most powerful tool any of us can possess.

"THE WATCHER", IVEAGH GARDENS

Mind and Body

Spas, natural therapies and yoga classes must lag just behind construction as the growth industries of the Dublin boom years. Typically, we tried to create quick-fix solutions to stress. An entire industry sprung up and suddenly massage tables and Ashtanga classes were the only places we could switch off and unwind. Which is nonsense, of course.

Taking care of oneself requires a little more than moving from the aromatherapy dispensary to the yoga mat. But if approached for the right reasons and not hurried, these time-out treatments can provide a useful foundation for a happy, healthier life; at the very least they're good ways to gift-wrap some sensory TLC.

Oriental arts and natural sciences have gone gangbusters as the grapevine resonates with stories of unconventional success, and complementary medicine becomes more broadly accepted. People are flocking to acupuncturists, naturopaths and other holistic healers, recognising that it's better to maintain the motor than try fixing it after a breakdown. When it comes to natural therapies, personal recommendations are the way to go. Failing that, see the lists of accredited practitioners on websites trying to regulate each association and discipline.

YOGA A sore back tempted Jennifer Keegan to give yoga a lash over 20 years ago and she's been practicing and teaching it ever since. "In the 80s it was really something that your mother would do in the local church hall wearing odd socks," she says with a touch of nostalgia for the lost innocence. She noticed things changing in the 90s when the pace of life accelerated and people were in a hurry to let off some steam. Aggressive, high-paced forms of yoga became dominant and some people really started to torture themselves into feeling healthy. More recently Jennifer has noticed a move to slower and softer forms. "The Dublin personality is not well adapted to stress, so there is a definite move back to deeper relaxation rather than just getting a buzz, says **Jennifer** *(Olive Tree Studios, 15 Grantham St; www.olivetreedublin.com; 087 285 3029)* who teaches a soft and reflective form.

In yoga, the teacher matters more than the studio, and we've compiled a list of recommended teachers whose approach to the ancient practice is about substance over style. **Caragh Eagan** *(Sunrise Yoga, Dún Laoghaire; www.sunrise.ie; 087 987 7552)* helps provide balance to stressful lifestyles through 'restorative' classes focusing on acceptance, tolerance and release. **Michele Van Valey** *(087 120 7695)* also teaches out of Sunrise, which is a lovely chilled-out space that welcomes the casual drop-in. She specialises in a gentle restorative form for older people, specifically aimed at alleviating suffering caused by ailments such as arthritis.

Aisling Guirke *(087 289 1664)* teaches Lyengar yoga, where the emphasis is on precision, correct alignment of the body and safety in each asana or posture. She teaches classes throughout the city. The teaching of **Tony Purcell** *(087 285 3029)* is infused with his great sense of humour, and he's been teaching gentle forms of Hatha and Ashtanga yoga for many a year around Dublin 4 and Dublin 8. He's also available for private classes if you're worried about the risk of letting one rip in company.

In an oasis of calm in the heart of Temple Bar, the inimitable **Greg Walsh** *(The Wooden Building, Cows Lane; www.samadhi.ie; 087 135 3095)* teaches Iyengar yoga. He was introduced to Yoga while travelling in Nepal and likes to see it as a tool for inner transformation and an aid to becoming more awake and aware in everything we do.

If you like the notion but aren't sure if yoga's your thing, try an introductory class (they're often free) with a school in your area. **Yoga Ireland** *(www.yoga-ireland.com)* explains the various different forms and has an extensive list of experts for the whole Dublin region. Beyond that, Colum Walsh's **Yoga Dublin Studios** *(Dartmouth Pl, Ranelagh; www.yogadublin.com; 4982284)* offers classes for everyone from beginners to experts, and prenatal mothers to parents with babies.

SPAS AND SALONS

The antithesis of slick, the contemplative and loosely Christian **Sanctuary** *(Stanhope St; www.sanctuary.ie; 670 5419)* would hate to be called a spa (if indeed, anyone there did 'hate').

It's a gentle, holistic centre built around an attractive, walled garden and dedicated to encouraging mindful living and a harmonious approach to modern life. At the same time they provide many marketable (and reasonably priced) tonics for our accelerated lifestyles including Shiatsu, full-body massage, Indian head massage and the perfect gift for a partner who never seems to listen, Hopi ear candling.

Massage, by the way, is one of the oldest of the healing arts, and dates back to 3000BC in Chinese history. Hippocrates himself, the father of medicine, recommended that all physicians be proficient in "rubbing techniques". Getting a massage treatment is one of the easiest ways to get a boost of endorphins through the sense of touch.

Many flash hotels have spas attached but boutique **La Stampa** *(35 Dawson St; www.lastampa.ie; 677 4444)* is probably primo, offering indulgent and sensory delights almost worthy of the hyperbolic brochure. Here they focus on Southeast and South Asian styles and have native experts in various treatments like Javanese Lulur, Thai and Balinese massage and Indian Shirodhara, a restorative therapy using warm aromatic oils on the forehead. They're all luxurious chill-out experiences worthy of a splurge, bettered only by an overnight stay in one of their sumptuous rooms afterwards.

Speaking of which, if your body needs a weekend away, **Solas Croí Eco Spa** *(Brandon House Hotel, New Ross, Co. Wexford; 051 447 333)* is a 90-minute drive from the city and the most eco-conscious of our hotel spas. Run on geothermal heating, woodchip boilers and solar energy, this spa bases its treatments on the ancient Indian science of Ayurveda, which is all about restoring personal balance.

And finally, how about a hair salon without a single hair product? Shane Boyd set up the exceedingly relaxed **Natural Cut** *(33/34 Wicklow St; 679 7130)* over 20 years ago and was about two decades before his time. While the styles are innovative, the method couldn't be simpler: just spray, rinse and cut.

MINDFUL MOVEMENT

Ta'i chi (or the 'unstoppable fist') is an ancient martial art, which was actually designed for self-defence but is more popularly practised these days to promote health, calm, suppleness and longevity. With the recent influx of Chinese immigrants to Dublin comes the familiar sight of practitioners in our public parks, and just watching this beautifully flowing, moving meditation is enough to slow down your heart rate.

If Ta'i chi might be your speed, visit www.taichi-ireland.com for a rundown on the associated benefits as well as a list of classes near you. A great way to start the day, and get your mind and body in sync, is to learn a few basic moves and practise them in your favourite outdoor space (or inside and near a window if it's raining).

MEDITATION

Given the amount of time we spend in our own heads – and the rare occasion when we get off them – it pays to invest in a little gentle refurbishment from time to time. Making space for positive thoughts is one of the most life-affirming things we can do.

Deserving special mention in this area is **Cultivate** *(15–19 Essex St West, www.cultivate.ie; 674 5773)*, a wonderfully innovative and holistic educational resource where you never know what might be on the mind-expanding menu. You can find peace with mantra meditation; aid your environment with 'how to make your own solar panel' classes; absorb some practical fruit gardening tips; or let your soul run free with Kirtan singing classes with the Natural Mystic Orchestra.

In some ways this whole book is a form of meditation; it's about promoting an everyday mindfulness that helps you slow down and feel grounded in the simple and most gratifying pleasures of Dublin right here and now.

Learning how to meditate – whether it's part of yoga, a martial art, staring at the waves or, ideally, doing precisely SFA – is the perfect tonic for coping with stress. Emptying your mind of unnecessary clutter does wonders to create clarity and provide perspective, two useful allies in the hurly-burly of city living. You don't need to become a devotee; just learning a simple exercise will help you feel centred. Just like any exercise, meditation gets easier and more beneficial the more you do it. And if your friends think you've lost your mind tell them, on the contrary, you've just found it again. Fugue the begrudgers!

Meditation is a central tenet of Buddhism and the **Dublin Buddhist Centre** *(5 James Joyce St; www.dublinbuddhistcentre.org; 817 8933)* is an especially welcoming not-for-profit place that teaches the most basic form of meditation, a technique known as the 'mindfulness of breathing'.

The **Tara Buddhist Centre** *(18 Long Lane; www.meditateireland.com; 707 8809)* is a long-established and flourishing Tibetan Buddhist community that offers meditation classes for all levels.

The relaxed but serious **Insight Meditation Group** *(www.insightmeditationdublin.com; 282 8199)* has been around for over 25 years and meets every Wednesday in Ballybrack for a meditation session followed by tea and a chat. It organises regular day and weekend retreats in the city and to surrounding counties.

Class Action

Think about something you like doing, and then do it more. Forget about self-improvement; focus on the fun or you'll never get around to taking that cookery, craft or life-drawing class you've talked about endlessly. Get a hobby, broaden your horizon and help yourself to a piece of me-pie. Here's a selective prompting guide.

ARTS AND CRAFTS

We love the unsupervised life-drawing classes at **Trinity Art Workshop** *(191 Pearse St; taw.csc.tcdlife.ie; 608 2725)* on Thursdays from 7–9pm. It costs €10 for the general public, and you can just rock up and start drawing without advance booking. If you feel like you need a little tutoring before drawing somebody else's bum, there's instruction available Tuesday evenings. If you want to hone your skills some more, the **National Centre of Art & Design** *(NCAD, Thomas St; www.ncad.ie; 636 4200)* offers 22-week courses for all skill levels.

Working with wet clay between your fingers has to be one of the most satisfying ways to, er, earth yourself and get in touch with your creative side. Trinity Arts Workshop and NCAD both run classes, and **Ceramics Ireland** *(www.ceramicsireland.org)* provides a list of recommended pottery and ceramics teachers around the city.

Lots of people rave about the jewellery-making course at **Yellow Brick Road** *(12 Lower Liffey St; www.yellowbrickroad.ie; 873 0177)*, which is suitable for beginners and people with a little experience. The eight-week course costs €250 and comprises 21 projects you make and bring home including wirework, crystal beading and spiral drop bracelet techniques.

The brilliant, generous and pioneering **Kaethe Burt O'Dea** *(compost@desireland.ie; 087 244 4185; see also page 122)* runs a traditional soap-making course from her house in Stoneybatter and sets a 'no-buy Christmas' as a useful goal. Kaethe and her friends make presents for each other rather than forking out cash to buy things that will probably end up as more waste. Soap is a great gift when you've made it with your own hands using old Irish methods and flavouring it with herbs from the garden. The one-day workshops are held on weekends in October, November and December.

COOKING

Nowhere do practical, creative and gratifying come together as easily as in the kitchen. A cooking lesson or two is the gift to yourself that will keep on giving, especially if it rouses a love of good slow food prepared and shared with care and delight.

That charming oasis of calm in the city, **The Cake Cafe** *(www.thecakecafe.ie)* runs a lovely little cookery course called The Perfect Dinner Party, which runs through Irish and seasonal specialities. Over three consecutive Mondays you'll be taken through three starter recipes, three mains and three desserts. More courses are planned, themed along the lines of slow food. Private classes can be arranged, which make for a delightful Saturday night out with friends. And as you'd expect, there's also an exceptional baking class that picks up where your ma' might have left off.

If you're after something more exotic to thrill palates and friends, **Fabulous Food Trails** *(44 Oakley Rd, Ranelagh; www.fabfoodtrails.com; 497 1245)* runs specialist cooking days with international chefs focusing on the culinary arts and traditions of different countries like Thailand, India and Japan (learning to roll your own maki rolls is a treat in itself).

The three Dublin convivia of **Slow Food Ireland** *(www.slowfoodireland.com)* run different classes, demonstrations and lectures all over the city year round; recent favourites included 'The Art of Tea and Old-Fashioned Cakes' and 'Boxty Demonstration'.

GARDENING

An endless source of slow pleasure can be getting down and dirty with nature in your own garden. The obvious resource for inspiration is the **Botanic Gardens** *(www.botanicgardens.ie)*, a city treasure that hosts lectures and demonstrations throughout the year and runs short seasonal courses on subjects ranging from composting to organic vegetable gardening and growing native plants.

The Sanctuary *(www.sancturary.ie)* is not just about spiritual growth; it runs an eight-week Organic Gardening course where you learn the basic techniques for growing veggies, fruits and herbs without chemicals. They, literally and metaphorically, help you sow the seeds that you can replant in your garden.

Permaculture, a sustainable method of gardening and growing food that is based on an understanding of natural systems, is starting to influence far-sighted Dublin gardeners. **Cultivate** *(www.cultivate.ie)* runs a permaculture class, but we really love the family nature centre **Carraig Dúlra** *(c/o Cahn, 4 St Laurence's Park, Wicklow Town; www.dulra.org)*, which hosts two-day introductory courses that show you how the principles can be applied to your own home or community garden.

MUSIC AND DANCE

The spiritual home of the uilleann pipes is probably at the vibrant **Na Píobairí Uilleann** *(Pipers Club, 15 Henrietta St; www.pipers.ie; 873 0093)* on beautiful old Henrietta St. Dedicated followers of old-fashioned, they maintain the traditions of the uilleann pipes, which started in Ireland around the beginning of the 18th century. They run classes in reed and pipe making, and provide tuition for all levels including stone-cold beginners.

The club is also home to the **Brooks Academy** *(www.setdance.com)*, established by a group of set dancers in 1982 and now with over 200 members and classes three times a week. Set dancing is one of our great communal, all-in-it-together activities, more about pleasure than precision. Classes are graded so newcomers won't feel out of their depth. And never did dances come with such handsome names; it'll put a special spring in your step when learning Clare Lancers, the Sliabh Luachra set or the Waltz Cotillon.

For just about every other style, you can take the first step with **Dance Ireland** *(Liberty Corner, Foley St; www.danceireland.ie; 855 8800)*, which offers a range of classes for all levels, including flamenco, jazz, contemporary, contact improvisation, swing and salsa.

A Day Disconnected

"You don't realise you're an addict until someone takes your drug away," writes Peter Souter, who runs the eco-travel website www.goodtravelcompany.com and agreed to pull off the information superhighway for a day without his electronic devices.

"I'm not a computer geek. I don't play shoot-'em-up games into the wee hours or get excited about the size of my hard drive. In fact, I'm probably your average techno Joe who uses the computer and internet for work and finds the mobile phone great for keeping in touch and texting occasional bad jokes. I won't miss my gadgets for a day, will I?

"The first thing that hits me when I wake up is that I have no idea what time it is. For years now my mornings have begun the same way, with the beep of my mobile's alarm clock. It prompts me to flick on the radio and RTÉ One's *Morning Ireland*, the woes of the world at high volume keeping me awake. Today is different; with no electronic aids I decided the night before to let myself wake naturally. I wake to silence. My wife Nik is still asleep beside me, breathing softly. Our 10-month-old daughter, Matilda, hasn't stirred yet. Must be before seven then. Am I programmed to wake early? Has technology rewired my body clock?

"Silence in my own house. How rare it is. No radio, no TV, no ringing phone, no computer purr. I hear a single bird warbling outside the window. He sounds like he's just doing it for the craic, just to let me know what I've been missing. Or perhaps he's poking fun at the absurdity of days that begin with rude electronic voices and the clutter of news reports and advertisement jingles.

"I finally hear Matilda stir and go into her room. She is sitting up, looking at me expectantly, ready for our morning ritual. I normally take her out of her cot, put on a CD compilation of African children's songs and watch her sway to the beat. A little self-consciously under her waiting gaze, I replace the electronic sound with the considerably less melodious tone of my voice as I attempt to sing her favourite Swahili songs, clicks and all. Matilda smiles and I start to get into it, throwing in a little shuffling dance move, and we both laugh. After a while her interest wanes and she waddles over and gives the CD player a few bangs. The message is clear; no day disconnected for her.

"I work from home running an eco-travel website, so most of my day is spent on the phone or online, checking emails and bookings. Working from home is a mixed blessing: I don't have to commute, but it's harder to switch off (my brain and the computer) and I often find myself checking messages well past bedtime. This morning at breakfast, in the unusual silence, I'm a little twitchy, hurrying to finish my toast. I realise I'm desperate to check any emails from the night before. Am I like this every morning? I know there are no urgent emails, nothing that can't wait a few hours at least; it's more the habit,

Shut down
Turn on silent
Lock keys
Normal
Meeting
In car
Select

an activity I'm compelled to do regardless of whether it is actually necessary or helpful.

"Noticing my edginess, Nik laughs at the fact that I am only an hour into my day disconnected and I'm already cold turkey. I laugh back, struck again by the absurdity of technology having such a pull over me. Let it go, I think to myself, forget about the unopened inbox. I focus on the crunch of my toast and the tang of the thickly spread marmalade. Thank the lord nobody has come up with virtual food...at least, not yet.

"I head into town with Matilda, surely a safe refuge from my cravings. Pushing the stroller, I catch myself over and over reaching for my phone to check the time. I left it at home, of course, and I feel suddenly liberated not having a clue what hour it is. I am truly disconnected now, wandering in time and space. We hit the park and spend hours – maybe – hand-clapping and playing peek-a-boo. I feel calm and unstressed. Matilda notices; she has my undivided attention, playtime without interruptions. I feel a twinge of guilt that she doesn't have it more often. Her drooping eyelids tell me it's time for her afternoon nap and I head to the child-friendly Bite of Life cafe, picking up a newspaper on the way. Now this is a simple pleasure. I read the paper back to front (sports first like a good Dub) without interruption while Matilda snoozes in peace. I used to do this every day, savouring a good half-hour with a broadsheet; when and why did I stop? Getting news off the net has turned it into just another activity to be done in front of my monitor. It strikes me that technology blurs the line between work and play.

"Having a baby makes evenings very busy – dinner, bath and bed. Shattered at the end of the day, Nik and I often watch a bit of TV and I feed my computer addiction with a laptop on my lap at the same time. There's just so much you can access off the net these days, so much potential, so much temptation, that it's easy to forget what I'm losing as a result. Free of my electronic distractions, I chat to Nik. She's still laughing at my struggle but I get the feeling she's enjoying the freedom of being disconnected as much as I am. 'I'm going to read,' she declares gleefully and runs upstairs to open a book she hasn't opened in weeks. That's where my day ends, sitting there and watching her read. And I've never felt more connected in my life."

> “ **TECHNOLOGY IS THE KNACK OF SO ARRANGING THE WORLD THAT WE DON'T HAVE TO EXPERIENCE IT.** ”
>
> Max Frisch

Soul

Perhaps life's not such a mystery after all, and the old adage that you get out what you put in best sums up the way the world works. So investing a little of ourselves into our surroundings, friends, lovers and family usually pays us back in spades, enriching our lives and warming our hearts. Whether you are nurturing a garden, a meal, a new pet or a relationship, they all work out better if you put in your heart and soul.

HOME We can't always live exactly where we want, and an apartment facing the motorway mightn't be the most uplifting place to come home to. But wherever we are, we can decide to make that place ours, stamp it with the imprint of our personality and fill it with a little warmth and soul. Gardening, cooking for friends and keeping pets are three traditional, uncomplicated but oft-overlooked ways to bring life and vitality into our living rooms.

Even in the greyest part of the city, a garden can soothe the soul and brighten our mood. TV gardeners might sell us images of idyllic country cottages with enough room for an orchard and a gaggle of free-range chickens, but in reality space is often at a premium in the city and a good old window box can be one of the best ways to express your creativity and tune yourself into the rhythm of nature. You'd be surprised what you can grow in a box or a big pot: tomatoes on a sunny balcony, peppery rocket by the bunch that replenishes itself after you pluck a few leaves, even garlic, chillies or a few spring onions.

Just don't bite off more than you can chew. Herbs are good starter plans, and the hardier ones like rosemary and thyme flourish in boxes. Garden centres will sell seeds and some of them have online ordering websites. Denise Dunne's **The Herb Garden** *(Forde-de-Fyne, Naul, Co. Dublin; www.theherbgarden.ie; 841 3907)* is a wonderful certified organic herb nursery in North County Dublin. They stock over 130 types of herb seed and give expert advice on what you should grow and when.

If your window box starts to take off and you want to get a little more serious about your gardening, **Dublin Food Growing** *(www.dublinfoodgrowing.org)*, **Cultivate** *(www.cultivate.ie)* and the **National Botanic Gardens' Herb Garden** *(www.botanicgardens.ie)* are three great resources aiming to promote food growing in the city and encourage Dubliners to get their hands dirty again.

And then, of course, the ultimate reward is cooking with ingredients from the garden and sharing it with friends and family, a communality that goes to the heart of the slow philosophy. Why leave it till Christmas and turn it into a chore? Invite your friends over early and get their input. Ask them to collect some thyme from the garden and put them to work picking, chopping and chatting.

See Class Action earlier in this chapter for a few choice cooking classes, or just dip into the old family repertoire and see what comes back to you. Lately, we've been reviving old family staples that somehow seeped into the subconscious and have been waiting patiently: coddle for Sunday morning breakfast, smoked fish poached on a Friday with hand-cut chips, homemade jam tarts baked on Saturday evenings, mince balls in crispy breadcrumbs for a quick snack. It's also nourishing for the soul to realise that this family heritage hasn't been lost by the generation of the convenience meal.

PETS

The first living creature Leopold Bloom converses with at the outset of his momentous day is, of course, his cat. "Milk for the pussens," he says, and the uncomplicated pleasure he gets from the closeness of the familiar animal in his kitchen is obvious and touching. Psychologists love telling us what we already know; a pet is good for the soul. The unconditional, uncomplicated love we give to and get back from an animal can keep isolation and loneliness at bay in the big city, or just add a little fun to family life.

Add to that by getting a pet that might otherwise be put down. Harsh, we know, but there's no point beating around the bush. Anne McEavor of **Animal Rescue Group** *(www.irishanimals.ie/dublin_homes.html; 289 5284)* sees this "double joy" that adopting a rescued pet brings. The group consists purely of volunteers who try to match abandoned or unwanted animals with stable homes. They work with a couple of sympathetic vets when neutering and vaccinating the animals. The Dublin branch of the **SPCA** *(Mount Venus Rd, Rathfarnham; www.dspca.ie; 493 5502)* has a Noah's Ark of a shelter that houses dogs, cats, cows, goats, donkeys, rabbits, snakes and a host of other animals dumped by their owners. They are all looking for new homes.

HEART

Now we go steady to the pictures
I always get chocolate stains on my pants
My father he's going crazy
Says I'm living in a trance
Thin Lizzy, 'Dancing in The Moonlight'

Dublin rocker Phil Lynott knew there was something special and transformative about 'going steady', taking your time to connect with another human being. It may make your head rush but it's best not to hurry affairs of the heart, which is why we prefer slow dates to shotgun weddings. Where speed dating has all the romance of an auction house, slow dates are all about doing something inventive, surprising and wonderful. There are some ground rules: simplicity is your friend on a slow date and you should be breathless with anticipation, not exhaustion. A bit of planning may help, but it shouldn't cost you an arm and a leg. Spending €100 at a French brasserie won't necessarily buy you a better time than doing something that's free but fun.

Fresh air and green spaces are a wonderful aphrodisiac, and the Phoenix Park is a lovers' playground. Renting a tandem from **Phoenix Park Bike Hire** *(www.phoenixparkbikehire.com; 086 265 6258)* at the city gates kicks the date off with a hint of romantic comedy and allows you to leisurely discover the best spots for a blanket-on-the-grass picnic in the shade or an afternoon of deer-watching. And if you're unlucky enough to have a row, at least you can't really ride away in a huff. The tearoom beside the zoo is a lovely spot to share a bun. Cap off your day with a hand-in-hand stroll around the perimeter of the zoo after it closes, stopping as you go to listen

to the noises of the animals at play and peer through the fence to spot a wolf, tiger or seal chilling after a day's entertaining. A swim in sultry **Vico Rock** is a chance to get half-naked with someone you fancy. Geeing each other up for the leap into the bracing water and then letting the sun dry you both off as you doze on the chalky rocks is a slow sensual delight to be shared.

In winter, seek out pubs with open fires – up in the mountains can be the best spot – or cook together after shopping at Temple Bar or Howth Farmers' Market. As local rockers Thin Lizzy said, a night at the pictures, especially if it's two seats at the back of the old-school Screen Cinema, chocolate stains and all, is still a classic, no-fuss couples night out. But coming up with something out of the ordinary makes for the perfect slow date. Instead of a hasty sandwich or coffee, meet for a lunchtime recital at the **National Concert Hall** *(Earlsfort Tce; www.nch.ie; 417 0077)* or share a few tears at a heart-wrenching evening opera at the beautifully restored and plush **Gaiety Theatre** *(South King St; www.gaietytheatre.com; 679 5622)*. Ah, go on.

In Other Words

Reading is essentially slow, and we all know grabbing a book is a healthy proposition for mind and soul. But sometimes we need a little help, encouragement or the threat of friends getting jacked off with us. Charlie Quinn, and many like him, found the solution in forming a book club. Charlie's runs monthly in the Blanchardstown Library *(Blanchardstown Centre; 890 5560)* where 20 members enjoy the camaraderie of a regular get-together and the invigoration of debate about the book they've all read. Just about every Dublin library hosts a club.

And of course there's hardly a more intimate way of getting to know your city – especially this city! – than by reading it as a character in literature. "When I die, Dublin will be written in my heart," said the life-long exile Joyce. Literary depictions begin and end with his masterpiece *Ulysses*, which of course only a few of us have read cover to cover.

Many other renowned local scribblers have waxed lyrical or turned poisoned pen about their hometown. Robert Nicholson is in charge of the collection at the Dublin Writers Museum and reels off his favourite Dublin moments in literature. He immediately recalls the caustic satirical view of the Free State capital in Beckett's *Murphy*, and particularly the scene in which Neary assaults the buttocks of Oliver Sheppard's statue of mythic hero Cúchulainn in the GPO.

Flann O'Brien's *At Swim-Two-Birds* is Robert's second suggestion, for its "glorious descriptions of Dublin pubs". Its hero is a student who spends more time drinking stout and lounging in bed than studying – hardly a work of fiction at all, then. And Dublin's greatest lovelorn poem is perhaps Kavanagh's 'On Raglan Road'. Pause and savour these couple of lines: "On Grafton Street in November we tripped lightly along the ledge/Of the deep ravine where can be seen the worth of passion's pledge." Did you hear Luke Kelly's voice in your head?

Urban Birdwatching

Taking interest in the passions of others can be a wonderful way of nourishing the soul and seeing the world anew. And when Northsider Eric Dempsey invited me out for a day's birdwatching, I couldn't resist, imagining – in my naivety – a pleasant stroll through the Phoenix Park to the accompaniment of warblers and thrushes and a bit of bird banter.

We meet early in the morning by the wind-bashed shores of North Bull Island on what turns out to be the coldest October day in years. A score of nondescript black and white birds bob on the rippling water and doubt creeps into my sleepy head; what in the name of Jaysus am I doing here?

Eric's smile warms me a little. Dressed for the occasion, he's puffed out in a fleece and insulated jacket, binoculars around his neck. I'm shivering in jeans and a ridiculously thin city coat. Probably taking pity on me, he suggests we sit in the car and wait for the tide to go out.

First lesson: birdwatching is governed by nature's clock and no other. In spring and summer birdwatchers head for the Dublin mountains to glimpse woodland and bog birds, preferably at dawn when they're singing their hearts out, making them easy to locate. In winter it's down to the sea for migrating birds that feed on Dublin's rich mudflats, revealing themselves only at low tide.

As we walk to the car Eric tells me to look out across the empty marshy grassland around us. "There are about 20,000 wading birds hunkered down in that grass right now," he says. I scan the desolate landscape, nod and think, 'yeah right'.

As soon as he starts talking birds, Eric reels me in. He has a knack for storytelling, which you can read in his popular book, *Birdwatching in Ireland* (Gill & Macmillan, 2008). "Birdwatching sounds like trainspotting," he says, "so we use the term 'birders' – a bit more macho." Twitchers are a whole different species, I learn. They feed off the information of patient birders about rare sightings then dash about spotting what they can, and jotting it down on their obsessive scorecard. The main thing birders do is wait. As the wind rocks the car and howls against the window I think I'm definitely more what is known as a 'dude', a casual birder who prefers pleasant surroundings and nice weather.

Almost self-consciously, I ask Eric about his favourite bird. "The swift," he says, without missing a beat. "After five weeks in its nest, let's say in the gutter of a garden shed in Glasnevin, weighing about 30 grams – a packet of crisps – and with a brain the size of a pea, the swift sets off on a 10,000-mile trip to somewhere in South Africa. And after two years he flies all the way home to exactly the same shed," says Eric, pausing to savour my giddy delight. "But here's the beauty: in all that time, two whole years, that bird hasn't stopped flying once. It feeds on the wing, even sleeps on the wing. You can't hear about the journey of the swift and not be amazed."

Time has passed unnoticed and I look out the window to see the tide has fallen back and the multitudes Eric promised have indeed come out to feed. We hop out of the car and he throws me a pair of 'bins' (binoculars apparently takes too long to say). A flock of Brent geese suddenly takes off from the water in perfect formation. Anticipating my question, Eric points to where a large grey heron flies low above the ground. "They saw his shadow and thought it was a falcon." Falcon? Now I'm hooked and alert, bins keenly pressed to my eyes.

I see something smaller and brilliant white flicker behind them. I focus in on a freakishly long and elegant neck, slim, jet-black beak and exuberant head plumage. Eric whispers the words "little egret". I stare, captivated. It is a warm-water, Mediterranean bird and Eric saw one of the first in Ireland in 1981. "Now there are around 800 breeding pairs." I don't need to ask why. I stay focused on the bird; its exotic form, incongruous against the cold landscape, brings home the reality of global warming. "Birds can fly," says Eric. "An oak tree can't just up and decide to move. But birds can and this makes them nature's register of change."

Eric's phone beeps with what turns out to be the most poetic text message I've ever read: "20 twite at Mallon Head". It's from a friend in Donegal and I get a window into the community of birders, the shared thrill and generosity of knowledge. Eric uses his phone to update the Birds of Ireland News Service *(BINS; www.birdsireland.com)*, an online resource providing tips on where to watch or twitch each day.

The tide has retreated further and the shoreline is suddenly fluttering with life. Eric intones the melodic names, "redwing, black-tailed godwit, widgeon". On the sand I notice a large specked shadow and look up to see a thousand-strong flock of small brown birds darting about directly overhead. "Golden plovers, just arriving probably," says Eric, his voice conveying a special affection for these beautiful, nervous birds. "Listen. We might hear their call." I hear the faintest 'plu-eee, plu-eee' from above, which Eric imitates instinctively. I'm thrilled by the thought of recognising that plover call next time.

When Eric goes for an evening walk in summer he hears the rolling call of different species of birds ahead warning each other about the upright creature approaching. What a way to experience the world, I marvel. The plovers land as one, and I see why they are so-called as I look out across a carpet of sun-catching, golden plumage.

Out of nowhere a man appears, bins around the neck, and greets Eric warmly. Another birder, Michael, has taken a few hours off work. He pulls out his battered notebook and informs us of two ringed geese he has seen today. He's read the code on their ringed feet and will later go online to look up their life history and flight path.

"Anything else?" asks Eric, never taking his eyes off the plovers. "A sparrow hawk on the rocks further up, causing mayhem as usual," says Michael. "Pat had a foster's tern yesterday, up by Clogherhead." Eric nods. He already knew. Michael heads off. To my delight I realise he mistook me for a fellow birdwatcher. You know; he might just be right.

ERIC DEMPSEY SETS HIS SIGHTS AT NORTH BULL ISLAND

play

FOR OUR AMUSEMENT

> “ *MAIREANN CROÍ ÉADROM A BHFAD.*
> **THE LIGHT HEART LIVES LONG.** ”
> Irish proverb

Televised sport is becoming so ubiquitous that it's starting to lose all meaning. Oh great, another 'must see' game, another 'Super Sunday' doubleheader. It all reeks of money-men, a desperate need to sell advertising and the transformation of singing supporters into couch-surfing consumers. Sport can be so much more, especially when it's local, leisurely or unique. In Dublin, it's an arena where we bond with our neighbours, maybe by joining the local GAA club, turning up to cheer (not scream) on the under-12 girls' soccer team or just getting together for a picnic while half-watching a cricket game on the lawns of Trinity College.

Even if you feel a little left out in this sports-mad city, surely you can't deny the simple joy sport brings, whether it's swaying in song with 10,000 other faithful fans on The Hill or taking a downright foolhardy jump into the 'Baltic' sea waters for a Christmas Day swim. At its core, after all, sport is no more than organised play, and an excuse to let the child in us run wild.

Local

We love the intense and gloriously inconsequential drama to sporting victory and defeat that allows us to compete with all our pumping hearts and then retire to the pub for drinks with the very same men and women we were trying to beat the lard out of a couple of hours before. And there's no better camaraderie than in the games entwined in our local heritage.

GAELIC GAMES Even if the GAA doesn't float your boat, you have to admire games that are local, inclusive, traditional, amateur and thriving. Don't you? Born in 1884 out of a political need to forge a national identity and culture, *Cumann Lúthchleas Gael* revived one long-dead game (hurling), completely contrived another (Gaelic football) and almost overnight made them the most popular pastimes in every parish in the country.

Dublin of course is primarily a **football** county, with hurling something we're more inclined to appreciate from a distance, specifically a safe distance. And we love to brag about it being the fastest field game in the world; a contradiction not lost on us slow coaches.

For most Jackeens, our experience is played out in a tragic, all-too-brief summer love affair with the county football team's triumphant march towards that elusive All-Ireland title. Early in June car aerials don navy and blue flags, pubs dig up their fading photos of the great teams of the 70s and 80s and the *Evening Herald* starts to get carried away with its back-page headlines of a "Blue Tidal Wave".

Then some Sunday in August, in a sold-out Croke Park (only the Dubs sell out Croker) it all goes horribly wrong and we curse management and tactics and shake our heads as Kerry stroll to another championship.

But for its club members and supporters, the magnificently democratic Dublin GAA – every member in every club has an equal vote in all decisions – is about so much more than cheering the Metropolitans from The Hill. GAA in Dublin is essentially a working-class game, and in its Northside suburban heartlands like Marino (St Vincents), Glasnevin (Na Fianna), Blanchardstown (St Brigids) and Ballymun (Kickhams), the GAA means culture, community, continuity and craic – replicating in pockets of the big smoke what happens in every parish in the country.

The guardians are doing mighty work protecting the culture of Gaelic games from the preposterously lucrative international sports with which they compete. And during the televised school finals of recent years, whose cockles haven't been warmed by the sight of sons and daughters of recent immigrants enjoying and excelling at our traditional games?

You don't even have to support a club to keep the spirit of GAA alive because the association's fifth official sport, perhaps the slowest of them all, is the hit and giggle of **Rounders**. It's still the perfect family game where kids bring the speed between the bases (or jumpers) and adults add a bit of oomph with the bat. So, when the weather warms, turn off the telly, gather some neighbours and do your bit for the country.

For Community and Club

"Once you play for a club that's it for life," club secretary Larry McCarthy shouts in my ear amid the back-slapping and cheering of clubhouse celebrations. Earlier that freezing morning we joined 200 fans on pilgrimage to watch Naomh Barróg's junior hurlers upset Rathoat of Meath in a final. The trip back was a small but loud convoy of horn-beeping and flag-waving D-reg vehicles.

Formed in 1974 by teacher Dick Fields, and squeezed between the Northside giants of St Vincents and Raheny, Barrógs of Kilbarrack thrive on being the scrappy underdog. "Kilbarrack was a rough neighbourhood back then and all the kids could do was kick a ball around the street. So Dick had a brainstorm and the club was born," grins Larry. "He wanted to get the old headmaster from Scoil Lorcáin enthusiastic about the club, so he might send some kids down. He knew he was a Mayo man, so went with the westerners colours of red and green." The relationship is still the lifeline of the club today.

Larry's face radiates pride as he surveys the unbridled joy in the packed bar that the volunteer-run club scrimped, saved and lobbied to build in 2001. "Some of them are second generation, their dads came up through the juniors in the 70s and 80s and now their own little kids are playing for the underage teams." Larry himself is a Barróg of 20 years' standing.

Days like this are rare at a small club, but vital to stoke the enthusiasm of members. "The club is not just about sport; it's about community, everyone volunteers and we look after our members. The clubhouse is a social focal point and we try to instil the love of Irish culture in local people." The Barrógs have over 400 social members, non-playing Kilbarrackeens who love the atmosphere, camaraderie and subsidised booze.

But old rivalries remain. Chelsea is playing Arsenal on the box; Larry shakes his head vehemently. "That wouldn't be on if Kirean [the club president] and I weren't away at the match." Competing with the hype and constant TV coverage of soccer, Dublin GAA clubs rely heavily on the success of the Dubs' senior team. "If they have a good run in the All-Ireland then we get more kids taking an interest." But as every fan knows, relying on the Dubs succeeding is like banking on sunshine in February. Instead the club invests heavily in its relationship with local schools.

Dublin clubs have unique character; Barrógs, for example, are underdogs, propelled by the prospect of beating big boys like Vincents and Na Fianna. But one thing all clubs have in common is a desire for more people to get involved. Just going along on a Sunday afternoon will boost club spirit. Look along the sideline at the *bainisteoirí* roaring encouragement and beyond them the fans – parents, siblings, friends and fans of the game. The amateur and democratic nature of the GAA means everyone involved has a voice. There is no 'them and us' within a GAA club; it belongs to you as soon as you walk in the door.

Although steeped in a long, local tradition, **handball** has hit a metaphorical wall over recent decades. There are records of Irishmen playing the game as far back as the 1520s, with religious authorities complaining about lowlifes enjoying the 'rebound game' against church walls. The game was hugely popular and even had an international dimension, with Irish immigrants exporting the game to the US and Australia. The best players joined a semi-professional circuit that saw a class of shenanigans that would make even Don King blush.

It was big news on the streets of Dublin when, in 1920 and at the height of the War of Independence, Ballymun boy Morgan Pembroke dethroned the great Johnny Bowles as Irish champion. No doubt Pembroke enjoyed some advantage in coming from a place where sizeable flat walls were aplenty. A few years later, the GAA adopted, formalised and 'amateurised' the game, which continued to blossom.

Doing their bit for the future of *Liathroid Láimhe* are GAA clubs like Na Fianna (the largest in the country), Naomh Padraig in Croke Park (the oldest in Dublin), and the Garda Club, which has the last outdoor court used in competition.

The recently reopened St Michan's Park, near the north end of Capel St, has a classic old outdoor handball alley for a game with an historical edge; Fatima Mansions residents are trying to revive a long-dormant handball tradition in their area; and it's high time for a renaissance around the rest of the capital. You can buy a handball at any decent sports shop; look up a few rules on the GAA's website, grab a mate, head to a wall and give it a crack.

COMMUNITY GAMES

Uniquely Irish and particularly slow, the community games have been going strong for more than 30 years and have the highest participation rate of any sporting or cultural activity in the country. They are inclusive, fun, grassroots, healthy and delightfully life-affirming.

For millions of Irish children the Community Games was and is their first introduction to an idea that sport is not just about watching United on Sky. Instead they join in and witness an outdoor fun event, run by people from their own community, where they get a chance to test out their awkward limbs and hear their hearts beat a little faster in running, throwing, kicking games where the focus is never on winning at someone else's expense. The neighbourhood's best six to 16 year olds in each sport go on to compete in county finals, then provincial finals and then on the nationals. But it never gets too serious or pressurised on the way, enjoying the same all-inclusive and celebratory spirit at every level. And don't worry if your kid isn't the fastest runner or fanciest dribbler; the organisation has widened its remit in recent years to include just about every pastime and hobby known to humankind (see www.communitygames.ie).

It's an independent, voluntary organisation that inspires 20,000 volunteers to provide games for young people in every county of Ireland, with about half a million participants at last count. There's probably an organisation near you, through a local school or community group. If not, what are you waiting for? This author wouldn't be a former 4x100m relay finalist if someone like you hadn't decided they could make a difference.

Leisurely

CRICKET "A game for skinny Southsiders who can't play rugby," is how our chip-on-the-shoulder friend from Blanchardstown describes a game of such exceptional slowness that it can take five days to play.

Once upon a time the summer sound of leather being thwacked off willow was to be heard from every corner and every class of the city. Cricket was played here as early as 1792, long before Association Football or the GAA were even dreamt of. By the mid-19th century it was the most important game in the city, with most parishes boasting a team. But the growth of the GAA, its ethnic cleansing of Irish sport and the ban of 'foreign games' killed off cricket among the lower classes, and the sport retreated to a few spectacularly beautiful ovals mainly – but not exclusively – south of the Liffey.

But the last 10 years and a softening of old prejudices have seen something of a cricket revival (despite Dubliner Ed Joyce, arguably our best player, defecting to England). The national team has produced some stunning victories (stunning Ireland as much as the cricketing world), which have stoked local interest. And an influx of cricket-mad Indians, Pakistanis, Aussies, Kiwis and South Africans has infected Dubliners with their passion and egalitarian approach to the game.

Our friend Santos George of Sandyford Cricket Club recommends the best way to appreciate the anachronistic, mellow rhythm of this fascinating sport is to take a picnic and spread yourself out on the grass beside the pastoral little square of **Phoenix Cricket Club** *(www.phoenixcricketclub.com)* in the Phoenix Park. This, would you believe it, is the second oldest club in the world and dates from 1830. One of its former members, a middle-order batsman named Charles Stewart Parnell, came to be known as the 'uncrowned king of Ireland' although history tells us that this was more to do with politics than his prowess at the crease.

Trinity College is another glorious place to watch a game as you sip a cool pint from The Pav. Your best bet is to bring along an expert, someone who can instruct you on the subtleties of this ancient game. You'll unlock the code of 'googlies' and 'the silly mid-on' and develop a deep affection for the game that, no matter whether it's played in Dublin or Delhi, unfailingly stops for tea.

LAWN BOWLS Okay, starter for 10 points: in what Dublin sport recently did a boy of 10 play seniors while a man of 94 played junior league? If there's an outdoor sport that requires less exertion than lawn bowls, then we're yet to find it. It's the epitome of slow and graceful; with the curve of the solid wood against your hand, the sun and breeze on your back, and the carpet-soft grass underfoot, enjoy a game that can take anything up to three hours to complete.

Shay Ryan, a veteran of the Bray club, loves the "simple sporting and social pleasure of a game where you can have a good long chat with your opponent between ends." The sport has been going for over 300 years in Dublin, when the first green was laid right in the city centre, just off College Green. Back then it was definitely a pastime for toffs but TV coverage and a conscious outreach effort have attracted wider and younger participation in recent years. Down-to-earth **Crumlin Bowling Club** *(831 3140)* offers free open days from April to June, where interested folks can come along, get a little coaching and try their hand at tossing a few woods.

FISHING One of the joys of fishing, surely, is the positive feeling that you're actually engaged in an activity while not doing very much at all. It's as much about finding a quiet natural spot for a bit of quality down-time as it is about matching your wits with a particularly tricky tench.

"I love getting away from it all," says Leixslip angler Colin Dunne. "I hunt out secluded spots, where you don't see a soul, I find these quiet places and I never tell anyone about them." Colin is a coarse fisherman, which doesn't refer to a stingy unwillingness to share choice spots, but rather the practise of fishing in rivers for non-game species like pike and perch. This is the most popular form of fishing in Dublin. What they catch they throw back, which is either the most sustainable form of fishing or a complete waste of time, depending on your perspective.

Of course there is an extreme element to angling, the polarity between the long, ponderous periods and the instant euphoria of ("Jesus Christ, hold my beer") actually snagging something. But calmness and serenity are the prevailing moods. We hope Colin won't blow a gasket if we mention a few sweet spots to cast a line and park your backside: along the Liffey up near Leixslip, further afield near Celbridge, on the Royal Canal near Ballybough, or in Memorial Park above Islandbridge.

Kicking Racism to the Wall

Bar none, the single most uplifting, man-I-love-Dublin day on the sporting calendar is the annual SARI Soccerfest. Sports Against Racism Ireland *(www.sari.ie)* is a clever, progressive community volunteer organisation that quickly realised the cross-cultural pulling power of sport and how it could be used to bring new immigrant communities together. For two days every September it takes over the Garda Sports Ground in the Phoenix Park and turns it into a festival of multicultural colour and chaos.

At the centre is a 48-team six-a-side tournament that is a wonderful clash of styles, with up-and-under native teams taking on the fancy footwork of Brazil, the precision passing of Poland and the mesmerising flair of Nigeria. The event has taken on a life of its own and grown beyond sport to become an annual highlight of local cultural diversity.

Lunacy

OPEN WATER SWIMMING

Only 'mad yokes' would swim in the bloody cold waters around Dublin, or so you might think. Open Water Swimming is not just a leisure activity in Dublin but an organised sport. It has a long and proud history as depicted by Jack B Yeats in his iconic 1923 painting, *The Liffey Swim*.

The Dublin Liffey Swim in September is still the highlight of the racing calendar, preceded by the Dún Laoghaire Harbour Swim in August, and lesser ones including at Portmarnock Beach and the Bray Promenade.

You'll certainly know you're alive, joining a few hundred brave citizens for a bracing swim, and we're not just talking about the shock to your system. But once in the water it gradually becomes a solitary slow experience, with all your senses brought to life, just you and the water and the beat of the stroke.

You can get more info from www.swimireland.ie but bear in mind that, to enter one of these open water races, you need to be a member of a swimming club and be able to swim at least a mile. See the next page for an account of a Christmas plunge at the Forty Foot.

CLIMBING

"I took a very dim view of climbing in the beginning," says John Goodall of www.climbing.ie; "pointless, dangerous, and for people wearing spandex, I reckoned. I had to be dragged along." At first it was the thrill of overcoming his fears that got John hooked, but "now, years on, the pleasure is in the middle bit, each move up the rock, every little victory over gravity," he waxes. Climbing for John is solitary and mindful, being in the moment and focusing on the rock. "Work, love, financial troubles all melt away once you tie that rope," he says. "But the real beauty of climbing for me is that there is no level you have to attain, no one pushing you, no one to disappoint or blame."

Most begin on an indoor climbing wall in larger gyms like **Westwood** *(westwood.hosting365.ie)*, **UCD** *(www.ucd.ie/sport)* and **Trinity** *(www.tcd.ie/sport)*. But they soon graduate to the natural – or is it manmade? – **Dalkey Quarry**. Carved out of the granite of Killiney Hill, the quarry is the hub and heartbeat of Dublin climbing, and has protected and varied routes that suit every level from beginner to pro. And for those who reach the top, a bonus reward is a spectacular view over Dublin Bay. The Dalkey climbers are a convivial lot and welcome any newcomer crazy enough to join.

Some younger climbers are into **Urban Bouldering** (you can connect with them through various pages on www.climbing.ie). These are the kind to carry around with them climbing shoes and a little hand chalk in case they stumble across a wall, arch or other city structure crying out to be climbed. Scaling Nine Arches Bridge in Milltown, the perimeter wall of the Royal Hospital Kilmainham or a granite wall at Marlay Park are a few of the more popular ways to get 'in touch' with your city.

Forty Foot Christmas

Walking down the steps to the sea, one part of my brain registers how clear the water is today; a green crystal against worn granite; how the bay curves around to Dún Laoghaire pier and behind it Howth. The other part of my brain is in shock and it soon takes over!

It's Christmas Day and the weather is perfect – beautifully still, not too cold, no, even a sniff of warmth in the air I imagine. I pass a steady stream of people walking back from the shore, towels underarm, all wet hair, smiles and Happy Christmases. They don't seem too cold, right? It's all good.

At Sandycove the place is hopping – and it's only 10am. There are charity stalls selling mulled wine and the Christmas tree glitters in front of the sea. As I make my way down the steps to the Forty Foot, I pass snatches of bravado-filled conversation: "Have a great one!", "The water's lovely", "Jesus, it seemed like a good idea in the pub last night!"

Down by the sea a woman wearing a Santa apron, hat and only togs underneath, is dishing out sandwiches to the family; a group of lads form a long line, arms round each other, shivering in shorts for the 'before picture'. Groups of coated observers stand around watching, there but not fully there, shoulders hunched as if feeling the cold themselves, shaking their heads and whispering, "You're mad!" It's hard to get a bit of space to change; everywhere towels pile on damp clothes and coats, so I stand at the edge where the sea brims for a while.

This rocky enclosure opens out into the sea – a perfect open-air bathing pool that always has glorious, deep water whatever the tide. *Ulysses* opens here, of course, with the "scrotum tightening...snot green sea". We are bounded on one side by high, almost sculpted rocks that are perfect for jumping off, but dangerous too, unless it is high tide and you know the underwater secrets.

It's 10.15am and a man takes a high leap off the rocks, all shout and limbs as he hits the water. A minute later there is the swing of his head as he shoots up, the sting on his face as it contorts into a smile and he swims rapidly to the steps with loud gasps and exhalations. On his way out he passes an older man who dips his hand in the water, blesses himself and serenely pushes off doing a leisurely backstroke around the 'pool'.

The queue going down into the sea is getting longer and so when a friend passes and confides that there is a bit of space round the back, the plan changes. I strip off to my togs and three of us head to Kavanaghs, a midway point between the Forty Foot and Sandycove, the tip of this small rocky promontory. Bare feet on granite, each step is a shock as soles contact stone, and we are quickly moving around the high wall of the old headquarters of the 40th Foot British regiment. This is where the place gets its name; the water isn't 40 feet deep as you'd suppose. This is the furthest thing from my mind as I hop from one rough-hewn step to the next, picking my feet up as though stung. Scotsman Bay opens out before us, the seafront with its candy-coloured houses, all yellows and pinks; the bay all dusty greys and bluey-greens – hard to tell where sky ends and sea begins – and the long arm of the pier behind it. I keep moving so I can't change my mind and now am standing at the top of the steps that lead into the water. I take a deep breath and jump; all thoughts turning instantly to pure sensation:

Sting of ice water – breath gone – move fast – oh good God – five strokes out – go on, one more – see the iron pole on the rocks ahead – now turn back – fast as I can – stinging skin – cold that burns – kind of getting used to it – never knew my arms could propel my body this fast – out of the water – exhale – climbing back up steps – didn't realise shins could feel cold! – back out on land.

My body has been stung to warmth; I am glowing, I'd forgotten that sensation of utter wellbeing after a swim, clear head and mind. All the same I have to keep moving and race back to my clothes, getting dressed as quickly as I can, unsure whether I feel damp, cold or warm, such is the adrenaline rush. Then I'm off to get some mulled apple juice, with a measure of something stronger and enjoy this Christmas fiesta, this giant outdoor party.

As I leave the Forty Foot, my blood singing, skin feeling as though it is has been doused in champagne, I pass a radio reporter and a press photographer on their way down. I remember the admonishment of a friend who is also a regular swimmer: "Make sure to write about all the other days down here!" I love Christmas Day but love more the day-to-dayness of the place; the camaraderie of winter swimming, the languid summer days with swims to Bulloch and talk of tides and flows and temperatures, of jellyfish and seals.

There are the different 'shifts': the seven o'clockers, (known to bring torches in winter); the nine o'clockers, mums who've just brought the kids to school; the 11 o'clockers whose members range from their 30s to 80s. They can always be heard from a distance, singing and laughing, and armed with flasks, cakes and bikkies until a periodic diet ripples through the group and it's all apples and grapes for a spell. Then there's the one o'clockers who include in their number the LDSs or Long Distance Swimmers and several winners of the Liffey Swim. If it's true that the best things for health and long life are laughter, the sea and friendship, it's all here at the Forty Foot.

I think of yesterday, Christmas Eve, a mild winter day too and I had just missed the 11 o'clockers – they sang carols for an hour. A couple of families had a party at Sandycove, it was even warm enough for the kids to paddle as parents shared out mince pies. Round at the Foot there were 10 or 11 people, everyone was full of tips on how to avoid the worst of the crowds today – "I'm coming down early", "What time is high tide Tommy?", "Carol said the rush was off by two last year". Before heading off to dive into the shops I stood and let the sea fill my eyes, perfectly calm, light spilling off it as the full tide brimmed against the granite. A pair in togs chatted and out beyond the Elephant Rock a cormorant rose, then dived for a fish, emerging a minute later sleekly black and empty beaked.

Nell Regan

motion

WAYS TO GO

“ **SLOW DOWN, YOU MOVE TOO FAST.**
YOU GOT TO MAKE THE MORNING LAST.
JUST KICKING DOWN THE COBBLESTONES.
LOOKING FOR FUN AND FEELIN' GROOVY...
LA-LA-LA-LAA-LAA-LAA...FEELIN' GROOVY. ”

Simon and Garfunkel

Indeed, life is like a long and winding road, as Father Trendy used to say. Except in this day and age, you've got some crazed commuter in a gas-guzzling four-by-four up your bum, beeping his horn, flashing his lights and making a bloody nuisance of himself. Go at his pace and you'll miss everything. The journey will be over before you know it, and you won't even remember what it was all about.

You've got two choices: risk crashing; or pull over, pause and proceed at your own pace. As important as getting somewhere is how we get there, and being master of our own momentum is paramount.

Slow Modes

In the grand scheme of things, how we get somewhere is as important as where we're going. It's a simple truth known to those enlightened souls that cycle, stroll or breeze past as we're stuck in traffic barely holding together. We asked a couple of light and merry travellers to guide us on the best ways to get about the city.

BY FOOT *Everywhere* is within walking distance, if we take the time. And who's ever regretted taking the time to walk? Strolling clears the head, stimulates creativity, slows down the heart rate and connects us to our little patch of the world more intimately than any other activity seems to.

If your destination is within your suburb, walk there. Map the area in your mind as you go, noticing the sights, smells, sounds and street names. If going further afield the public transport/walking combo is a great idea, with the DART especially useful for opening up all the coastal walks. Adventurous Dublin stroller Siobhan O'Keefe, who hooks up with an informal group for regular walks around the city, highlights a few inspiring paths.

Anywhere along the beach will reward but Siobhan has a special *grá* for **North Bull Island**, with the long strand of Dollymount and the wild sand dunes behind it. It's only a few steps from busy Seafield Rd and across a century-old wooden bridge, but it feels like a great escape. "You can walk along the sand dunes going out and along the beach coming back. What I love most is the mixture of natural and old Dublin industrial, the thousands of wild birds on the mudflats and the large Sandymount chimneys rising up in the background.

"But easily my favourite," she says, "is the **Head of Howth** because it is still incredibly wild for a city walk." Follow the loop around the cliffs as they hug the coast, and let it take you down to wonderful inlets and coves along the way. You'll forget you are in the city with wildflowers on the cliff edge, seals swimming offshore, and views out to sea over Lambay Island.

"I did the walk by myself the other week on a beautiful clear day and I didn't see another soul for the first hour and a half." The coves are a great place to stop for a private picnic and you pass two Martello towers on the way. "Arriving back in Howth is another great part of the walk, with so many lovely places to refuel and grab supplies, including the weekend farmers' market."

The **Bray to Greystones Cliff Walk** begins on the seaside promenade of Bray village before turning out over the cliffs. Siobhan enjoys the fact that the 8km walk "cuts through a huge variety of wildlife and hedgerows, and past some breathtaking coastal scenery." **Bray Head** is a much simpler up-and-down walk on the iconic hill on the edge of town. It's a long-standing local tradition to get to the top of the head at least once in your life, and on a clear day you can peer into the heart of the Wicklow Mountains or all the way to the coast of Wales.

BY PEDAL

Cycling expands your perception of place and allows you to see things you'd never notice in a car. In the zone, it's a great way to empty your mind of petty anxieties and feel connected with the natural world.

Everyone should cycle now and then, if only to see how the other half lives (ie, perilously). Organisations like Dublin Cycling Campaign **Dublin Cycling Campaign** *(home.connect.ie/dcc)*, which organises regular 'social bike rides' in and around the city, we've become more bike-conscious. **Dublinbikes.ie** runs Dublin City Council's brilliant new bike rental scheme with 40 location between the two canals to pick up or drop off one of the shiny (for the moment at least) new bikes. You need to register online for €10 but the bikes are free for the first half hour and only 50 cents per half hour after that. Cycling in the city is definitely cool; just look at all the politicians pedalling towards the bandwagon.

Each year in late summer, the city rolls with the **Dublin City Cycle** *(www.dublincitycycle.ie)*, which deliberately slows down the streets with a leisurely mass family cycle on a circuit around some of the more beautiful parts of the city centre.

Also featured in our Gather chapter, Kieran Byrne of the inspirational **Squarewheel Cycleworks** *(21 Temple Lane South; 679 0838)* is at the forefront of promoting cycling as sustainable transport in Dublin and is the best resource for all things relating to rothars.

"I love how close we are to the mountains," says cycling enthusiast Frankie Levalle. "You can get there in under an hour, hardly see a car or anybody at all, and then be back in your house before you know it. There's always a little village nearby to get a cup of coffee, and to rest or warm up." Frankie was good enough to share a few of his favourite loops, and counts **Dundrum to Glencree** as one of his favourites. It starts off easy enough but then climbs uphill all the way to Johnnie Fox's pub in Glencullen, a great place to stop if your feeling it a little (or even if you're not). Savour the views before heading on to beautiful Glencree. Beside a stream there's a tiny graveyard for German soldiers who died in Ireland or in Irish waters, which makes an interesting and peaceful stop. "If you're up to it you can head up to the stunning Sally Gape," suggests Frankie. "Or else, like me, skip that and cruise all the way down to Rathfarnham, taking in the city panorama as you go."

For a gentler spin on the Northside, Frankie favours the **Phoenix Park and Strawberry Beds**, "basically through the park and then along a road that runs next to the Liffey all the way to Lucan." If you don't want to cycle through town, you can hire a bike near the entrance to the park opposite Heuston Station *(www.phoenixparkbikehire.com)*. Begin with a loop of the park on the outer road, and savour the sights, sounds and wildlife.

Then turn left off the main road and follow Furze Rd all the way to Knockmaroon Hill and into the Strawberry Beds, a route that has beautiful views of the river and the weir and feels almost rural. Frankie loves a couple of pubs on this route like the Strawberry Hall and the Angler's Rest, both old Dublin inns on the river with a good pint and a tasty toasted sandwich.

The **Howth Rd** along the coast and the **Royal Canal Towpath** from Phibsboro are another two scenic routes, both equally good for a stroll and, yes, Frankie assures us, there are a few good pubs along the way.

BY WATER Perhaps the calmest and yet most invigorating way of getting around Dublin is by boat – along the coast, up and down the Liffey or chugging along canals. The movement and sound of bow through water alone is likely to lull you into a more relaxed state. Being able to handle a kayak opens up the full wonder of our waterways to a leisurely commute; they are small enough to go into the tightest nooks and crannies, yet fast and durable enough to cover some distance.

Canoe Ireland *(www.canoe.ie)* runs introductory adult and junior courses at its exceedingly picturesque training centre where the Liffey bends in the Strawberry Beds. Once you've got your confidence up, at your slow command will be the entire river and canal network from Dublin all the way into the heart of Ireland.

If you want to head in the other direction, **Deep Blue Sea Kayaking** *(www.deepblueseakayaking.com)* runs sea kayaking courses offshore at Seapoint, the most sheltered part of Dublin Bay. Then they take you south around Dalkey Island and the Muglins (seal and seabird havens) before heading back to shore.

If you prefer something requiring minimum effort and maximum opportunity for daydreaming, Chris Lawless *(280 0915)* and Monica Smyth *(280 6517)* both hire small **rowing boats** out of Bullock Harbour in summer. You need at least two people and can head out to meet the resident seals or cast a line into the water and have mackerel for tea.

Sailing has been a Dublin passion since time immemorial and there is something quite primordially thrilling about harnessing the power of the wind and manipulating its currents to be propelled across waves. We have over a dozen sailing clubs dotted around the bay and on up as far as Skerries. If you've never before found your sea legs, lessons in a single-handed Laser Class are a great place to start, and available from each club.

Sailing in Dublin *(www.sailingindublin.ie)* is a clever, friendly little club based in Dún Laoghaire, which offers loads of opportunity to sail even without your own boat. They have a fleet of dinghies and two yachts for sailing activities and competitions available for all members. Beginners can sail with experienced crew on their Sigma and Ruffian keelboats.

If you ever get a chance to jump aboard an elegant Howth Seventeen Footer at **Howth Yacht Club** *(www.hyc.ie)*, you'll really sail through history. Walter Boyd designed the boat at Howth House, a stone's throw from the harbour, in 1897. Only 17 of them survive today, fussed over and raced weekly by their passionate owners. If you're feeling adventurous you could contact the club and see if you can help crew one for a day.

BY TRAIN A must-do for locals and visitors alike is an afternoon ride on the DART from Greystones around the bay to Howth. It is a train ride to treasure with an almost constant view of the sea mixed in with a cosy, box-seat lesson in local topography.

Incredulously, we meet lots of inland Dubliners who have never experienced the summer joy of a long, lazy, destinationless trip on the empty, gently rocking green train, with built-in stops for a swim at Killiney beach and an ice cream from good old Teddy's in Bray.

BY BUS We don't usually associate city buses with adventure (slow, yes; adventure? Not so much), but have you ever tried jumping on a random bus and seeing where it takes you?

Our roulette ball landed on the Number Two, and we spent an hour and a half enjoying a bird's-eye view of the old Dublin inner suburbs of Irishtown, Ringsend and Sandymount. The views swept from tight streets of neat, artisan cottages to wide roads, open coastline and the grand seaside three-storey mansions of Sandymount. And, of course, buses always take you back to where you started from, eventually, in the circle of city life.

The **31B** is another great ride along the northern coast road through working class Fairview, Raheny and Kilbarrack before beginning a wonderful circular jaunt around Howth Head, culminating in great views from the summit. Jump off in Howth village for a seafood snack and a walk along the strand before hopping on the next bus back home.

If you have a few hours to wander by public transport (here we like to think of 'transport' as that magical verb of transformation), then the **44** will take you up Townsend St into the heart of the city centre and all the way on to Enniskerry and the relative wilds of the Wicklow Mountains. Bring a packed lunch and enjoy the brick-and-mortar history of your city as you pass from the Georgian perfection of Merrion Square to the Victorian neatness of Ranelagh and then the hyper-modern boomtowns of Dundrum and Sandyford. When you hit Stepaside and the foot of the mountains, the climb begins to wooded Kiltiernan and finally the lovely village in the hills that is Enniskerry.

Tuk Tuk

A riddle. How do you combine innate laziness, an empty purse and ecologically sound behaviour when you want to make your way around Dublin's busy streets? Why, take a tuk tuk.

They are actually called eco cabs (www.ecocabs.ie), and you've probably noticed these pedal-powered carriages weaving between the traffic in the city centre each day, and wondered what they're all about.

"People are often unsure about our eco cabs," says super-fit eco cab driver Dave Lennon, "thinking we must charge a fortune, but rides are free and paid for by the advertising we carry. We carry anyone, tourists heading to Trinity or Dublin Castle, tired shoppers who just don't feel like walking anymore or students who are out mucking around. People love it, we are giving them a free ride after all. It's hard on the legs," he says, "but, man, you get fit pretty quickly." Uh, we can only imagine, Dave.

35

A Trip on the Daniel Day

Although not partciularly scenic, at least not in a conventional sense, there is something calming about the slow, silent progress the silver trams make through the crazed city centre – in the afternoon when the carriages are not full – that makes it a soothing way to sit back and have a look at your city without being caught up in the mad rush of it all. The two lines follow extremely different routes, each seeming to capture opposite sides of wealth, class and history in the city. The 'working class' Red Line stops at stations with names like Rialto, Fatima, Red Cow and Tallaght; while Windy Harbour, Stephen's Green and Beechwood hint at the Green Line's more upmarket neighbourhoods.

Tales from the Towpath

Bill Matthews is a "semi retired, mostly sedentary, former paper-pusher". He took a few days out of his autumn to stroll the 85 miles of the Grand Canal from Dublin to the River Shannon, a slow adventure he describes here.

I walked the canal on my own. That's the way I like to go. When I walk with someone I get caught up in conversation and lose sight of my surroundings. I also like to control my own pace, to be able to stop and see what I want to see.

Sometimes my mood is elevated and I walk faster, feeling the air in my lungs; at other times I might like to sit on a rock and gaze out over the landscape. And after being alone all day I relish all the more evening times in the pub or communal breakfasts around the table of a B&B.

Day One: Dock-construction debris stopped me from getting closer than 30 yards to the sea lock that separates Ringsend Basin from the Liffey. That would have to do. I climbed aboard an abandoned barge in the water and took a photo of myself; evidence – this was me at the very beginning of the Grand Canal.

For the first hour I walked a paved path, passing through the varied urban landscapes of Dublin – the old warehouse district, modern commercial developments, middle-class residential estates and poorly-maintained government flats.

Some parts of the city towpath were beautifully maintained by neighbourhood groups, proud of this exceptional amenity in their midst. One arched bridge after another carried the city's traffic overhead and I counted seven locks on the two-mile stretch from the Basin to Portobello.

Slowly, as the afternoon progressed, the environment started to change; the factories and warehouses of human development fell away to be replaced by open fields.

About a mile past lock 11 the real countryside emerged: golden wheat fields, cattle and sheep looking back at me as they chewed on lush grass, and this is where I had my first views of the Dublin and Wicklow Mountains to the south. I heard birds in the old hardwood trees that suddenly popped up along the banks before me. I spotted a group of blue herons at the water's edge, always waiting to see if I was continuing toward them before casually lifting their wings and flying a little bit further on, squawking at me for the disturbance.

Because I was down at eye level, walking, I could take all these magical things in. The country pleasures kept on coming as now the towpath was lined with blackberry bushes and I couldn't help stopping to collect the juiciest ones.

I felt good, not too tired; I noticed even at this early stage how the flat Grand Canal was gentle on a hiker, the grassy surfaced towpath easing the impact of the tens of thousands of footsteps.

Day Two: I crossed the Leinster Aqueduct and headed into the Kildare village of Robertstown on a quiet Friday afternoon. I approached the first local I met and asked about options for lunch. The Barge pub was his very appropriate suggestion, and a Greek salad and a pint of Guinness (yes, the combo worked) set me up for the leg to come.

Perhaps it was an engineer's joke, but the high point of the canal is actually in a place called Lowtown where the Old Barrow Line and the Main Barrow Line flow into the Grand. The towpath here was wide and grassy and I was in the swing of it, moving along without much effort. At the Bond Bridge I popped into Allenwood for a couple of quick pastries to keep me going. I asked the lady about a nearby B&B and was told there might be one 20 minutes on.

So I continued westward on the canal path, relishing the exceptional warm and sunny autumn weather. It was midlands peat bog country, flat with low-lying hills visible in the distance. Quietness and solitude surrounded me; I saw no one for miles and only heard the songs of playful birds and the sound of my feet on the grassy path.

As early evening fell the thought of lodging was on my mind – no B&B had been spotted. Maybe the evening air was getting to me, but I began to wonder if I could just hike all night and caught myself grinning at the audaciousness of it.

There was no sign of a village or a stray lodging, so on I walked. As dusk took over, then night, I paced soft and easy under a starlit sky, oblivious to the weight of my backpack. I slowed my pace as it got darker, becoming intensely conscious of the rhythm of my footsteps.

At about mile 44 I noticed cloud cover was slowly spreading overhead, extinguishing the last of the starlight, and walking became tricky. I was calm, unworried. A tall sycamore tree stood between the canal and the towpath. The ground under it was dry and covered in lush grass. After putting on some extra clothes and a big woollen jumper I settled into the soft grass just a few feet from the water. I slept.

Day Three: Shortly after dawn I woke to overcast skies that cleared as the morning progressed. The canal was narrow and dead straight as I set off and the waterway almost disappeared into the horizon a few miles ahead. My day's walk suddenly looked a little daunting. I was soon hungry and was delighted to spot the town of Daingean, where I bought myself a little picnic in the grocery store and ate it on the stone wall of Molesworth Bridge.

All through the day I walked, resting frequently under bridges with a half hour nap under the Bord na Mona railway bridge near mile 53. I was woken by the sound of fishermen setting up their gear for an afternoon on the canal.

The remainder of the walk to Tullamore was through bog and farm and past small cottages. The water of the canal seemed to show the grey cast of the bogfields runoff. Bury Bridge signalled my arrival in Tullamore and I saw my first barge on the canal, late-season holiday-makers who had rented the boat in town and were heading off for their own adventure. Over a slow pint, a town bartender recommended a little family-run B&B.

Day Four: After a huge breakfast, my gracious host, Martin, was good enough to drive me back to the canal and I struck out for Pollagh. For the first time since I left Dublin the weather let me down and it started to drizzle. Nothing too heavy, nothing I couldn't manage once I put on the rain gear. In fact, the rain was so light as I walked that only the stippled water in the canal told me it was still falling.

The countryside now seemed more remote than ever, with only a couple of farm buildings scattered here and there. I crossed over tiny streams and two aqueducts, and from one of these got a clear view of the ruins of Ballycowan Castle, built in 1626 and now standing forlornly beside a farmer's barn and out-buildings.

My shins had started to hurt the day before and so Pollagh was a modest target for the day. I saw the town's church spire in the early afternoon and headed for Gallagher's Bar. I asked if they served food. They didn't, the barman told me, but quickly added he could fix me up a sandwich and some soup. A few minutes later a homemade fresh ham sandwich and a bowl of vegetable soup arrived, and man did it hit the spot.

Day Five: To complete the Grand Canal walk I had to reach Shannon Harbour, a modest little town lying right where the canal hits the Shannon River, 12 miles away. But by the time I hit Ferbane the shins had gotten a little worse. I had to fix my mind on my goal and took little notice of my surroundings. But I was glad to pass the old bridges of Belmont and L'Estrange, as they were only a short hop from my destination.

The grandest sight on the whole walk had to be the old buildings and docked boats of Shannon Harbour looming in the distance. I had walked the Grand Canal! Although the canal, by its nature, doesn't pass through the flair and drama of Ireland's legendary mountains and coastlines, its landscape possesses a quiet and serene beauty that is mighty good for the soul. I felt a deep sense of spirituality there, alone with just the birds and the still waters.

travel

PLACES TO REACH

> “ THINK YOU’RE ESCAPING AND RUN INTO YOURSELF. LONGEST WAY ROUND IS THE SHORTEST WAY HOME. ”
>
> James Joyce

We’ve spent plenty of time celebrating the good, slow times to be had in Dublin, but one of the best things about living in the capital of somewhere so beautiful and varied is the opportunity and lure to get out. On a light traffic day – or even better on the train – two hours in any direction can transport you to a different world of natural delights. From ancient tombs and deserted islands, bucolic countryside and still winter lakes, mystical boglands to tree-thick mountains, there are more opportunities for weekends away than there are weekends to actually go away.

Going somewhere new changes our mindset; free of everyday constraints, we seem to create more time to delight in the small and the slow. Every escape from routine is a deliberately slow pursuit – some, we suggest, are just a little slower than others.

SLOW

Time Out

Fionn Davenport is a dear old friend of ours, and he's also the Lonely Planet writer for Dublin and Ireland. We asked him to nominate a few of the places he likes to go for a city break. When he's not writing about travel or researching for others, he tends towards quietness, emptiness and natural beauty, choosing places and seasons to avoid the crowds.

"When you visit any place is critical," says Fionn. "Somewhere that is overrun with visitors and bustle in July can be a sanctuary of solitude and nature in January."

LOUGHCREW

"My favourite place is Loughcrew in County Meath. It's home to the Loughcrew Cairns, which are 5000-year-old passage graves. Yes, just like Newgrange, but these have been virtually untouched by archaeologists and largely ignored by just about everyone else.

"Some amateurs excavated them in the early 20th century and removed a lot of the artefacts, so the place seems to have been forgotten by mainstream history and the tourism machine. Gloriously. There are no guides, no tickets, no coaches in the parking lot, no shop selling souvenirs, nothing at all like that; you can literally stroll up and have the place to yourself, and it's completely free.

"There's a little visitor centre up at the elegant Loughcrew Gardens *(www.loughcrew.com; 049 854 1356)* nearby, where you can borrow (there's a deposit, but no charge) the key to Cairn T. Yes, you can actually go inside. To get the most out of the place you might like to do a little reading beforehand, to stimulate your imagination, but you can walk freely and quietly – let's not forget *quietly* – among these earliest monuments to the first flickers of civilisation in Ireland.

"I tend to come here on winter mornings, when the light is at its most impressive and you can see and hear for miles around. I've never seen anybody else there, not a soul. In a world where all of the historic treasures have been catalogued and noted, exploited and controlled, we have this untouched, calm, mysterious place just a few miles out of Dublin."

COOLEY PENINSULA

"Because it straddles the border, there's still a bit of reluctance in Dublin about heading up to the Cooley Peninsula," says Fionn. "But it is one of the most atmospheric landscapes to explore on a fine winter weekend when beautiful Carlingford Lough is quiet and empty and the dark Mourne Mountains rise up all around you.

"In the summer it's full of water-sporters and Northees out for pleasure drives, but you won't find many of them around after October, when the place falls still.

"All the tales of Cúchulainn in the *Táin Bó Cuailnge* are set here and it certainly feels like epic country, with the mountains meeting the sea and old castles and dolmens punctuating the landscape. I find it a very romantic landscape, not picture-postcard cute, but dark and wild and beautiful, especially on a crisp morning if you go for a walk in the mountains and the hills around the pretty town of Carlingford. There are loads of great trails to follow and certainly in the cooler months, when the less hardy are indoors, you'll have them pretty much to yourself.

"And I have to recommend **Ghan House** *(Carlingford; www.ghanhouse.com; 042 937 3682)* to stay in if you want to keep that relaxed, romantic glow. It's an 18th-century house at the foot of Slieve Foy with walled grounds, big open fireplaces and views across the Lough. They have a cosy restaurant where they bake their own bread and use veggies and herbs from the gardens. They usually feature Cooley lamb, Carlingford oysters, and local cured bacon and free-range eggs for breakfast."

WICKLOW MOUNTAINS

"The single greatest gift nature has bestowed on the Dublin working stiff is the Wicklow Mountains. Within an hour of a jam-packed Grafton St you can be on top of Ballinrush Hill looking down at a panorama of mountains sweeping down to Lough Dan and catching sight of a peregrine falcon circling above your head for prey.

"I'm not sure we truly appreciate what we have, such unspoilt landscape so close to the city, and the accessible **Wicklow Way** *(www.wicklowway.com)* is a route full of adventure and exploration for leisurely long days and weekends away.

"You can begin in suburban Rathfarnham and take it all 127km to the Carlow village of Clonegal. Of course, most of us just dip into it, doing a few kilometres here and there, but there is added pleasure in staying overnight in some little inn or country house and seeing the Way anew the next morn. It's like a silent guide, taking you through the heart of our most varied natural world and through some of our most historically and mythically rich landscapes.

"Perhaps surprisingly, **Glendalough** *(www.heritageireland.ie)* is still one of my favourite spots to head on a free day, but only in winter. The summer crowds are just too much, and you can't appreciate what makes the place so special. But off-season, on a cold, clear day, I can totally understand why St Kevin chose the place for his get-away-from-it-all hermitage.

"I'm fascinated with the idea of a monastic retreat. When you take the steep walk from the Lower Lake up to the isolated Upper Lake, you start to leave the stress of city living behind you and open up to your surroundings. So by the time you arrive at the top, you're really ready for the wonderful views out over the wooded valley. I like to sit on the big rock and just look, letting my eyes and mind wander.

"If you're after a longer and more contemplative break, consider spending a night or two in one of the five Cillins, or little hermitages, at the **Glendalough Hermitage** *(www.hermitage.dublindiocese.ie)*, a non-denominational retreat run by the local parish. These are basically little no-frills, no-electricity cottages with a bed and open fire. For a nominal fee you can stay and experience some serious solitude."

Thanks for the inside track well-travelled Fionn; now please steer the tourists in the opposite direction.

DUBLIN'S ISLANDS

It's often said that travel is about the journey as much as the destination. In that case then, surely, a trip across water to a deserted island must be up there among the best adventures.

We rhapsodise about visiting islands off the west coast, but how many of us consider hopping across to an island off Dublin? (Apart from Britain, smart arse.) The islands in our bay are pristine, overlooked and mostly unexplored pockets of history and nature.

Many of them – like **Rockabill** and **Colt** islands off Skerries for example – are little more than big rocks teeming with wild birds and sunbathing seals. Some of the more precious ones are protected natural habitats. If you have a friend with a boat, a leisurely trip skirting the islands off Skerries is a thrilling chance to see exotic wildlife so close to the city. With a bit of persuading, one of the local fishermen or sailors might take you out in summer.

Lambay Island is privately owned (by the Baring family, whose bank went bankrupt in 1995 after rogue trader Nick Leeson made one withdrawal too many) and is certainly more than a rock; in fact at 2.5sq km it's big enough for a good stroll. It lies about 5km off Portraine and is accessible, with prior permission from the island steward only, from Rogerstown Harbour. Again a non-landing trip around the island in a boat may be the best option, with the chance of a gawk at the adapted medieval castle and Edwin Lutyens-designed estate.

But the big attraction is the wildlife; the island is home to a seabird colony of tens of thousands of guillemots, kittiwakes, razorbills, puffins, fulmars and many more. Throw in our only east coast colony of grey seals, a herd of introduced fallow dear and even a few wallabies – whose ancestors were exiled to the island in the 1980s from an overcrowded Dublin Zoo – and any sail-by visit would guarantee some very special Dublin sights. Once again, the right approach to a boatman in Skerries or Rush might get you a trip out.

You can definitely get out to the picturesque, uninhabited and evocatively named **Ireland's Eye** off Howth, at least in the summer. It's another impressive bird sanctuary, but also has an inviting sandy beach, a Martello tower and the ancient ruins of the 8th-century church of the Three Sons of Nessan. Island Ferries *(booking@islandferries.net; 086 845 9154)* run regular boats from the East Pier in Howth in summer.

On the Southside, **Dalkey Island** is another easy waterborne adventure away from the city and into the solitude of the uninhabited. There's another Martello tower, old Christian ruins and, of course, wild birds, but the real star attractions are the herd of wild goats who surely live the most isolated life of any Dubliner. Just head to Bullock Harbour in summer and look out for ad-hoc signs for boats to the island.

> **“ I TRAVEL NOT TO GO ANYWHERE, BUT TO GO. I TRAVEL FOR TRAVEL'S SAKE. THE GREAT AFFAIR IS TO MOVE. ”**
>
> Robert Louis Stevenson

Holiday at Home

Picture your travels in Dublin over the last week, imagining the ground you've covered shaded on a map. Like most of us, you probably took the same routes to the same places on the same days by the same means. Perhaps during your undeviating week you imagined a holiday – after you've cleared this busy period of that frigging debt.

But what's stopping you taking a holiday right now, taking some time for yourself and discovering Dublin anew? Block out slow time on your calendar, 'negotiate' a mental health day from work, and embrace Dublin as if for the first time.

Detour. Turn off the main road and explore a new suburb; get off the train or tram a few stops before you normally do and walk.

Hop on a random bus (if you don't like your destination, it'll return soon enough).

Avoid people you know for a spell, and seek out ones you don't.

Visit a new bar; eavesdrop on the locals; take the city's pulse.

Just like you've done on countless holidays, imagine what it must be like to live here.

Send postcards to friends about your holiday in Dublin.

Make your way through the city using only lanes and alleyways.

Leave buildings by the back or side door and see where they take you.

Get lost.

Visit tourist attractions you've been curious about but never actually experienced.

Tag along with a tour group and listen for free (until you're chased off).

Book yourself into a city hotel.

Ask friends for tips on new places to go (or, better, old places you've never been before).

Gather like-minded friends, mix up your keys and distribute them randomly. Spend the weekend at whatever house you get the keys for (what were you thinking?).

Journey into Space

When you get caught up thinking the world revolves around you, take a journey into space. The first time you see the moon through a telescope – ideally as it reaches first quarter – is unforgettable. It is fascinating to explore its pocked and creviced surface and imagine the moon controlling the tides, the groundwater table beneath our feet and perhaps, apocryphally, our own moods. Looking into space is a glorious way to feel small, not a bad thing every now and then.

David Moore, chairman of **Astronomy Ireland** *(www.astronomy.ie; 847 0777)* is proud that its Dublin branch "is the largest astronomy society in the world per capita, which means Dublin has the largest percentage of astronomers in the world." He attributes our fondness for all things stellar to the cloudy weather, which means that "when the stars come out, people get excited". Of course, our long attachment to astronomy goes back at least to the people who built **Newgrange** *(www.newgrange.com)*; and **Dunsink Observatory** *(Castleknock; www.dias.ie; 662 1333)*, opened in 1785, is one of the oldest in Europe. "It was the Hubble of its day," David says of Dunsink, "and astronomers from all over the world would come to use the telescope".

One of the most illuminating, grounding and underappreciated Dublin trips is to the observatory's free open nights on the first and third Wednesdays of each month during winter, when you can view heavenly objects through the historic Grubb Telescope. Astronomy Ireland holds many star-gazing events of its own in the Phoenix Park, near the papal cross, where there are few artificial lights to block out the view. Winter is the best time because of the long dark nights, but you need to dress warm. "The stars are seasonal," adds David, "for example some, like Orion, are only visible in winter, while you'll only see Sagittarius in the summer." Stay in touch with the website to find out what's happening in the skies throughout the year, and don't forget to check out the 'sobering thought' on the menu for some perspective.

BARGING Rather than dash through traffic on the *way* to your city escape (for two-nights-a-full-day-and-a-morning before you return to work), make the way your holiday by cruising out of the city along our majestically still canals. **Royal Canal Cruisers** *(www.royalcanalcruisers.com; 820 5263)*, based at the 12th Lock on the Royal Canal in Castleknock, rents out beautiful steel barges fully equipped with cooking and sleeping facilities. Their first punters (is that a pun?) in 1997 got as far as Kilcock, nearly 50km, in a week before they had to turn back, so bad was the state of the neglected Northside waterway at the time. How things have changed. Now you can take the pristine canal all the way to Mullingar, stopping as you please at pub and inn, and having the truly slow pleasure of shepherding your craft through the gushing locks along the way.

There is something serene about how a barge moves through the water; the measured pace and peacefulness lulls everyone on board into chilled-out bliss. The old industrial craft still hold a great deal of romance, and total strangers feel the urge to wave to you as you inch on by.

A further spur of the canal can take you to Longford Town and, any day now, plans will be hatched to reconnect the canal to the Shannon for the first time since 1960. The barge sleeps up to six and is a great way to take visiting friends through the city and on out the other side. The **Inland Waterways Association of Ireland** *(www.iwai.ie)* has a great guide to the canal route with notes on the locks, historic sights, towns and flora and fauna you'll encounter on your slow boat to, well, wherever it is.

small

SLOW THINGS FOR KIDS

“ **THE MOST EFFECTIVE KIND OF EDUCATION IS THAT A CHILD SHOULD PLAY AMONGST LOVELY THINGS.** ”

Plato

They're usually the ones racing around frantically, but children also have a wonderful knack for propelling us into the slow lane and simplifying life. They'll stop suddenly to pick up some choice autumn leaves or a particularly smooth pebble on the beach. They'll spot the moon or the first star when we are concentrating on mundane tasks like putting out the bins. Their determination to walk along a random wall, or dance up the steps of some public building, forces us to change our pace, even our objectives. They teach us patience and the benefits of going with the flow.

Seeing things as a child does goes to the heart of the slow philosophy. Feeling pure and uncomplicated joy, delighting in the small things, being quick to wonder and slow to lose our innocence are all things to which we should aspire. Rather than overanalysing everything, surrender to the instinct and imagination of kids, pick the fuchsia on the way home from school and admire the 'wiggly worms' as you go.

Thrills, Chills and Spills

We called in the experts in our exploration of Little Dublin, recruiting Aisling Grimley, mother of researchers Anna Rose (13), Kate (11), Eva (8) and Louisa (2) who took over this chapter and suggested occasions and activities that are good for everybody's spirit.

HOME

Wherever you are, children are a terrific excuse to play and be frivolous. You can start by making your own fun at home. Erect a tent, zip yourselves in and tell ghost stories by torchlight. Bake bread from scratch, or pick wild blackberries in season and make a delicious tart. Plant herbs in a terracotta pot and start a nature table for found objects like a bird's nest, peculiar twig or a daisy chain. Life cycles have a wonderful way of putting things into perspective.

After a week of school, sport, music practice, homework and getting in and out of the car, there's nothing like rushing into the backyard and staying put. Turn your tent into a yurt by filling it with as many scatter cushions as you can find. Wrap up in a blanket and lie on the grass counting the evening stars as they blink awake. Paint a flowerpot, dry flowers in a book, make cards with dried flowers. Talk Dad into frying cocktail sausages on the portable gas ring and eat them with little sticks, the grease running down your wrists and onto the lawn. Count the different species of birds that visit your garden and get a book from the local library that will help you identify each one.

Feed the birds and offer them a shallow tray for a bath and a drink. Then stand back and admire as they busy themselves eating nuts, seeds and leftover breadcrumbs or porridge. Plant seeds whether or not you have a large garden. In fact, a very enjoyable way to garden is by keeping it small and using a large window box or terracotta pot. Plant some bright, eye-catching flowers like sunflowers, marigolds and nasturtiums. Vegetables like radishes, lettuce and cherry tomatoes are also easy and thrilling for children to watch grow (see page 139 in Nurture).

PARKS AND PLAYGROUNDS

You don't need a book to tell you that kids love the great outdoors, or that their natural enjoyment of open green spaces can be enhanced immeasurably with a little imagination and wonderful fact. For the latter, visit **ENFO** *(St Andrew St; www.enfo.ie)* in person or online. It has lots of fascinating material and activities geared towards children, and a little prior research can really turn the outdoors into an adventure. (It's also a great refuge if the going gets tough on a trip into town.)

An outing to any half-decent Dublin park can be transformed into something special with a little creative thinking. Make an event of it, with before and after elements that will enrich the experience. A few slow games and activities on the way to keep the kids amused might be a good idea. It could be as simple as some timeless 'I spy' or some nature questions and riddles that will be answered by investigating the natural world of the park.

Seasonal trips to the same park open up opportunities to compare and contrast how the trees, plants, birds, animals and indeed people change their habits as the natural cycle progresses. Let them come up with ideas for things to collect and bring home, like acorns, conkers, or leaves and wildflowers for pressing. 'Plant craft' is a great way to continue the fun at home – you could make a picture frame from twigs, a bird feeder from pinecones or a mobile out of different-coloured autumn leaves.

Phoenix Park is every parent's best dig-out pal. We all have our own glowing memories of the place and it's home to two kiddies' standards: the zoo and an all-ages playground. But the top attraction for us is the opportunity to wander aimlessly for hours through its enormous, meandering expanses. Let the kids take the lead and walk, scoot or cycle the random paths that crisscross the grounds. Look out for a herd of fallow deer; jump into a pile of leaves gathered up for you by the wind; identify common birds by their song ('Robin!'); check out a lazy cricket game or the dramatic hustle of polo ponies in full flight; stroll through the beautifully planted walled kitchen garden before stopping off at the visitor centre for a bowl of homemade soup.

A more tamed but no less magical and private a place is **Iveagh Gardens**, a marvel of pure simplicity and beauty. There is no playground, just a walled 'secret garden' that tickles the dream world of children and is rich in story. Tell them that the waterfall has samples of rock from every one of Ireland's 32 counties, and mention the elephant that is buried beneath the central dugout area. He was in the circus and died during treatment at the UCD Veterinary College, which used to be in nearby Earlsfort Tce. Picnics on the grass and rolling down the small hill are favourite activities here, and the tree and bush surrounded fringes are made for spontaneous games of hide and seek.

Perhaps surprisingly, kids love the **National Botanic Gardens** *(Glasnevin Rd; www.botanicgardens.ie; 837 4388)*, particularly in summer. Visits start with a rush of excitement at the sheer variety of colours, textures and scents of the herbaceous border, but the real excitement starts when the first squirrels are spotted running and skipping through the ancient native trees. The October Halloween Parade is a treat, when children get to parade in their costumes through the decorated gardens.

The king of Dublin playgrounds is in the picturesque grounds of **Malahide Castle** *(Malahide; www.malahidecastle.com; 846 2184)*. The adventure area has a very tall slide at its centre, which is surrounded by a spider climbing-frame, a tyre seesaw and two button-seat rides that whoosh along a taut wire.

Of course, like any decent castle, this one is haunted. One story revolves around a painting that used to hang in the Great Hall of the castle. It featured an extraordinarily beautiful and anonymous lady in a long, flowing white dress. Everybody used to admire her, perhaps too much because one day she just left the painting and was last seen wandering around the castle. Can anyone see the white lady? If that doesn't get their little hearts pumping, pretending to get lost together in the woods next door might.

In **Bushy Park** *(Terenure)*, keen eyes can look out for the stunningly beautiful kingfishers that breed along the banks of the

Dodder. You'll need to get them into wildlife spy mode, treading very softly and looking out sharply in the wilder part of the park at the back. The playground is small but the unadulterated joy of tumbling down the big rolling hill is the real hit during summer. Bushy also has one of the few skate parks in the city and younger kids love to stop and gawk at the 'cool' older kids doing their tricks.

Rathfarnham Castle Park and Playground *(Rathfarnham; www.heritageireland.ie; 493 9462)* has loads of jungle climbing-walls and slides and swings of all sizes. Look out for the 'camera' on the climbing bridge where mirrors are used to reflect parents on the ground. There's also a more challenging natural log playground for older children in the woods just beyond the pond. The castle cafe is open for very tasty home-cooked scones, soups and sandwiches.

The beautiful beech hedge surrounding the playground at **Cabinteely Park** *(Cabinteely, just off the N11)* makes you feel like you're cut off from the world. The playground was designed by Richard Webb, an expert on play for children with disabilities, and uniquely caters for children of all abilities. Features include a willow tunnel and maze for a natural, sensory experience. The nearby wildflower meadow, best seen in the late lazy days of summer, is a perfect slow attraction of scent, sight and the sound of bees.

Marlay Park, in the foothills of the Wicklow Mountains, has two playgrounds, one featuring a mini assault course with a rope bridge, tunnel and climbing frames. There are delightful tearooms that lead into a magical walled garden with perfectly trained peach, plum, pear and apple trees (their produce is sold in the same tearooms in season).

DUBLIN ZOO

Let's be clear, Dublin Zoo qualifies as slow *mornings* only, when it's at its most magical, memorable and mellow. If you are among the first through the gates at 9.30am you'll be rewarded with an altogether enriching experience. The zoo is passionate about its conservation efforts and if the rate of procreation is any measure of contentment, then the animals here are very happy indeed.

The animals seem most receptive, curious even, at the beginning of the day when they're being served breakfast before the hordes of Homo sapiens arrive. In the stillness of the early hours, you'll hear their morning calls. There is something particularly cute about watching big cats wake, stretch out and let out a first gentle roar. The connection with the tigers can feel so intimate that you might catch yourself instinctively reaching to protect your kids.

The Swinging Gibbons sing in the morning to announce themselves in the wild, the huge balloons swelling under their chins a remarkable sight to see. Your kids will be transfixed. The elephants are best in the mornings too, playing and frolicking in the sand, the young ones nuzzling and the older ones nudging them towards the water for their morning 'face, hands and teeth'. If you're lucky you'll be there when the doors open, and the elephants charge out in a herd delighted to feast on vegetables and bamboo. In the uncharacteristic quiet of mornings in the zoo, you can hear them crunch on sugar beet. The exotic red panda are usually only active in the mornings, as they tend to snooze away the rest of the day. You'll see them come crawling down out of the trees (where they sleep) and catch the cubs at their friskiest.

Must-Have Memberships

- The Zoo Family Pass: repays itself after a couple of visits and allows you to see the changing zoo in all four seasons.
- Airfield House: farm, gardens, arts, classes or just hanging out and walking, Airfield provides options every weekend of the year.
- Mailing Lists: The Ark, Farmleigh, IMMA and Hugh Lane kids' clubs are great for keeping you informed of upcoming fun things for kids.

CITY FARM Never work with children or animals – oh, but play with them together as much as you can. Animals bring out the best in kids, and interaction with wild and domestic creatures is a wonderful big sensory dose of the smelly, living, barking or mewing natural world.

The noble aim of **Airfield House** *(www.airfield.ie; 298 4301; children/adults €3/€6)* is to "respond to nature, our traditions, and the rhythms of the seasons to ignite our sense of natural curiosity, wonderment, and playfulness". Sounds like a slow goal to us! Located in an old, big-house estate in the heart of thoroughly suburban Dundrum, Airfield was inspired by the open-minded and nature-mad Overend sisters, the last residents of the place.

The farm and natural habitat are designed to educate and delight, and the introductory Meet the Animals tour with real-life farmer Eamon Younge succeeds on both counts. Kids can join the Green Wellies Club, which meets Saturday mornings, to help Eamon with the feeding, breeding and bedding down of animals for winter.

But even if you're only visiting for an afternoon, you'll love stumbling across this hidden green world that feels like kids' fantasy and animal husbandry rolled into one. Sights and activities are seasonal, making it ideal for return visits to gauge the passing of the natural year. Children just melt at the springtime sight of a day-old lamb in the sheep pen, the younger ponies trotting in the paddock beside the main house or watching the progress of the tadpoles in the ponds. Fans of creepy-crawlies are encouraged to 'Bee a Nature Detective', and find out the mysteries of the insect world. Airfield is jam-packed with activities to ignite a child's natural wonder.

Airfield is also passionate about education and its place in the community, working closely with local schools and planting over 2000 native trees and starting a new wet woodland area aimed at attracting more wild animals to the vicinity.

SEASIDE Whatever the weather, a day at the beach is a winner. Most of our beaches are very kid-friendly and a dip in the bracing Irish Sea is a memory they'll cherish (but maybe not right away!). There's always a different focus of interest and wonder, from smelly seaweed to super-smooth shells, crazy gulls to chasing waves, and mysterious washed-up flotsam to thrilling seal and dolphin spotting.

Sandymount Strand provides a great walk, particularly at low tide when it teems with sea birds wheeling and wisping, and the sand is soft enough for digging and investigating. The large inlet of water that remains at low tide is known as 'cockle lake'. Tell them about the pirates who once hovered off Howth and made daring dashes into the harbour at nearby Poolbeg.

Balbriggan is another great wide beach for a walk (and run) and we like spotting and naming the different seabirds that turn up throughout the year. **Donabate** has the slidiest dunes and is best for hide and seek; **Killiney Beach** is never crowded and a great place to collect weird and wonderful shells; **Bullock Harbour** is the place to spot seals, drawn as they are by the local fishermen's leftovers. There's always a hint of adventure here, watching the men prepare their nets, head out to sea and return to empty their catch on the dock. It's a great reminder of Dublin's seafaring traditions.

WALKING Let's not, in our quest for new, overlook the simple pleasure of walking and feeling intimately connected with our little patch of the world. Children often require coaxing but they love it once they get going, particularly if you've rounded up some other kids for company.

Walking anywhere can be adventurous if you're in a slow frame of mind, but if you need a destination, start off with fairly flat walks like the **Grand Canal Milltown Feeder**. Beginning at Lowtown, it's an 8km path through one of the most pleasant stretches of county Kildare, taking in serene countryside, quarries, old mills, ancient ruins and a whole lot of nature along the way.

Progress to more adventurous uphillers like **Massey Woods** (accessible from Military Rd, about 6km south of Rathfarnham), which features a huge variety of trees and has plenty of picnic tables. Or the steep route up to the spectacular views from the **Hellfire Club** (from the car park off the R115 at Kilakee), regaling your kids with not-too-scary ghost stories along the way.

But king of the walks in our house is the (Great) **Sugar Loaf** of East Wicklow. Young kids and a mountain? Are you mad? The Sugar Loaf is really a gradual and manageable steep walk rather than a climb, but kids don't stand on technicalities and will love the lungful of mountain air, sense of achievement and proud story to tell at school on Monday. It only takes about 45 minutes to 'scale the summit', although some little legs may need help with the final ascent (the slightly shaley section at the end). The peak is 501m high and, isolated as it is, affords magnificent views stretching to the coastline. A picnic and a windy photograph are a must before your descent.

Another underappreciated adventure is to the reservoirs of **Bohernabreena** ('the road of the fairy hostel') which, although less than 20km from the city centre, feel positively enchanting in their rustic appeal. Two reservoirs were built here in the 19th century and still supply homes in the local area with, they'll tell you, the best drinking water in the world.

Take the R114 through Firhouse to Glenasmole and the entrance to the reservoirs. You'll hardly encounter another soul (which is just as well because parking is minimal). Glenasmole means 'valley of the thrushes' and if you spot or hear a thrush, wonder if its ancestors were around when Fionn MacCool wrestled in this valley, or when Oisín took off from these parts on his way to Tír na nÓg!

Take a picnic and amble at your leisure, exploring life in the hedgerows along the way. The area is planted with pines and larches; and reeds and willows have seeded themselves and provide great habitats for young birdwatchers to watch. Listen out for the increasingly rare sound of a song thrush, which repeats parts of its melodic tune twice (to be sure, to be sure perhaps).

Allow at least an hour for the walk itself and plenty more time for doddering (speaking of which, the Dodder River rises here). You will see all manner of spill tanks, weirs and other extraordinary water works as you walk along, especially between the upper and lower reservoirs. In August, bring a bucket for blackberries and make jam and crumble together when you get home. There are few activities more simple or joyful than cooking food you've collected yourselves and turning it into sweet, sticky treats (even if you might be horrified by how much sugar goes in!).

MUSEUMS AND GALLERIES

Although rarely top of a child's to do list, visits to museums and galleries work wonders as long as you keep them interesting, lively and short. Take an audio guide if it's offered because they'll prefer the independence of wandering at their own pace and being directly addressed by the guide (as well as pressing all the buttons).

The **Chester Beatty Library** *(Dublin Castle; www.cbl.ie; 407 0750)* is situated in a castle, which is a whopping big plus in the 'knights and damsels' world of a kid's imagination. The circular grassy garden out front is a great place for them to run about, playing in the simple little maze as you sit on the bench ignoring, sorry, *admiring* them and your surroundings.

Looking at the incredible collection of beautifully illustrated books, manuscripts and other religious art in the library itself, you'll be amazed how much our kids know about world religions through their primary school curriculum. The Silk Worm Club organises art and multicultural events for six to 11 year olds, including Sparkly Chimes where everyone makes their own Christmas decorations based on the museum's collection. The annual African Day provides a wonderful, intercultural riot of costumes, dance, food, music, traditional children's braiding and face painting.

With no prior booking required, Sunday Sketching at the **Hugh Lane Gallery** *(Parnell Square North; www.hughlane.ie; 222 5550; 3–4pm; ages 7+)* is a failsafe weekend activity when the whim takes you. The Saturday Workshops *(3–4pm; 6–10 year olds)* bring in local artists for fun classes like designing your own birthday or Christmas collage cards. The **Garden of Remembrance**, across the road, provides either a peaceful retreat or a welcome spot for a runaround after an hour or two sketching. Kids love the enormous bronze sculpture of the Children of Lir, a great excuse to launch into telling them one of our most exciting ancient Irish myths; they'll pay special attention to swans after that!

A giant old-school dolls' house might be the best way to describe **Number 29** *(29 Lower Fitzwilliam St; www.esb.ie/numbertwentynine; 702 6165)*, a brilliant introduction to the history of Dublin. The perfectly restored and fully furnished Georgian house shows how some (very privileged) children lived in Dublin in the late 18th century. The guided tour is excellent, and the period toys and the children's nursery in the attic a certain highlight. We were fascinated to learn how life was lived with no electricity for fridges, lights, heating or even PlayStations. A follow-up half-day at home without using electricity or running water is a fun lesson in historical empathy.

CLASSES AND ACTIVITES

Lining them up for out-of-school activities and classes doesn't have to turn them into clock-watching, over-timetabled mini employees. A few slow interests can ignite ideas and dreams they'll want to explore in their own time. The wide expanses of **IMMA** *(Royal Hospital Kilmainham; www.imma.ie; 612 9900)* and the genteel **National Gallery** *(Merrion Square West; www.nationalgallery.ie; 661 5133)* are two great, chilled-out cultural spots that put a lot of effort into their children's activities and are handy for rainy days.

Art and nature coexist beautifully at the **Pine Forest Art Centre** *(Glencullen, Kilternan; www.pineforestartcentre.com; 294 1220)*, which hosts two-week summer camps, Easter and Halloween courses and regular Thursday afternoon classes. In the inspiring natural surroundings of forest, river and mountain, kids choose between painting, sculpting, pottery-making, weaving, batik and paper crafts. Activities take place outdoors, weather permitting, and forest trail walks and natural material scavenger hunts spark endless ideas for later art play. There are courses for juniors (five to 12 years) and seniors (13 to 16), and everything is carefully supervised and tends to run smoothly. Private buses pick the kids up and drop them home every day, which makes up much of the €250–€300 cost of two-week courses.

The old grounds and elegant estate house, stables and gardens of **Farmleigh** *(Phoenix Park; www.farmleigh.ie; 815 5981)* are magical, as if designed by a child as a cool place to play. The first thing we do is collect windfalls in the garden and feed them to the two donkeys nearby. Activities at the old house are organised according to season, which makes this another great spot for return visits.

Eddie Lenihan is a masterful storyteller and a local treasure, who moves seamlessly from slapstick to suspense. Kids adore his take on old Irish lore, and his Farmleigh appearances around Christmas and Halloween are experiences to cherish. The Easter Sunday egg hunt is another seasonal special and marks the day with a riot of fun mixed in with a dose of tradition. The live crib with real animals is another thrill for the little ones.

A Checklist

No matter how much we tried to explain that lists were 'fast', our researchers insisted on listing their favourite slow things to do in Dublin.

- Wrap up well and walk or cycle down the boardwalk in Clontarf.
- Put on your wellies and splash in puddles in St Anne's Park.
- Kick and crunch the leaves in Bushy Park, collect conkers in Phoenix Park and feed the ducks in St Stephen's Green.
- Sit beside Paddy Kavanagh on his bench near Baggot Street Bridge.
- Pick blackberries at Bohernabreena and make jam.
- Watch the fishermen feed the seals at Bullock Harbour.
- Eat Burdock's chips out of the bag.
- Feed the birds in your garden.
- Go to a League of Ireland soccer game.
- Create your own family traditions: the Sugar Loaf on the last day of school holidays, Halloween at Airfield...you decide.

gather

SHOPPING WITH SOUL

> “**NOWADAYS PEOPLE KNOW THE PRICE OF EVERYTHING AND THE VALUE OF NOTHING.**”
>
> Oscar Wilde

With money being a bit tighter these days, there's all the more reason to make shopping soulful, sociable and fun. Countless small businesses and traditional stores have disappeared because of our appetite for global trends and compulsion for 'convenience'. The more it happens, the higher price we pay culturally, collectively and individually. So instead of allowing ourselves to be corralled into sterile malls and sold mass-produced dross by surly, uninterested staff (maaaah!), let's shop with our hearts, seek out places with soul and reclaim retail.

Whether it's a hand-printed scarf, a piece of 70s vinyl or an art deco vintage ring, buying something from a tailor, artist, collector or even corner shop helps to stimulate local creativity, puts money into the community and goes a long way towards taking the 'con' out of consuming. It's also so much more fulfilling to chat with people who are passionate about what they're peddling and who will bend over backwards to support you, the conscientious and contented customer. Be more than the digits on your credit card.

TEMPLE BAR
SRÁID CHÓP
COPE STREET
2
HIP HOP
SOUL/FUNK
ROCK/INDIE
TECHNO/HOUSE
REGGAE
JAZZ/BLUES
BEATS
DJ TOOLS
and more...
FREEBIR
RECORDS
ticketmaster
New/2nd hand
CDs & LPs
DUBSTEP
ROCK/INDIE
SOUL/FUNK

Reclaim Retail

Isn't it positively ludicrous that 'shopping' (you know, the luxury of buying stuff we probably don't necessarily need) sometimes feels like a chore? Try shopping the old-fashioned way: bring a friend and make an occasion of it; plan a relaxed pit-stop on the way; linger over something that has been handmade; talk to the person who made it (or is at least passionate about what they're selling). Only ever buy things you love.

Shopping

From frivolous to formal, recycled to cutting edge, this city is bursting with stylish creations to suit every purse and there's no reason not to wear local threads.

FASHION Tracy Tucker's family has been involved in Dublin's rag trade for generations, and the experience and local wisdom garnered is embodied at its classy little shop **Costume** *(10 Castle Market; 679 4188)*. It's run by Tracy, her sister Anne and mother Billie who, contrasting with their contemporary fashions, make sure customers get a very old-school, full-service treatment.

"It's almost like an old shop down the country," says Tracy. "There's no hurry, no hard sell, just calm and relaxed attention and expert advice if you want it." They carry rare international lines as well as many top local Irish designers including Vivien Walsh and Helen James. Pride of place, though, goes to Leigh Lee, the beautifully detailed designs of the younger Tucker daughter, who specialises in made-to-order for women.

Tracy cast an expert eye over her hometown and gave us a few tips on where to find local designers doing their own thing; "the fashion markets," she reckons, are the first place to look for Dublin creativity and independent, give-it-a-go design.

The **Loft Market** *(www.myspace.com/theloftmarket)* appears magically on top of the Powerscourt Towncentre, Friday to Sunday and for two weeks in the lead-up to Christmas. The loose-knit (excuse the pun) gathering of new designers brings a burst of fresh, young, eco-conscious savvy to the local scene. Blink Blink works with recycled objects to create rings and bracelets (we particularly like the ones with old typewriter keys). Kirby and Myler reconstructs and embellishes vintage clothing to create unique pieces, while Béibhinn Flood adds delightful hand-sewn beading and embroidery to her womenswear, which can be made to order.

The Saturday **Cows Lane Market** *(Cows Lane, Temple Bar; 677 2255)* is an outdoor summer market that has recently found an indoor winter home in SS Michael and John Banquet Hall *(Essex St West, Temple Bar)*. Accessories are its strong point with lots of inventive jewellery designers, along with a growing number of painters and craftsfolk.

Petria Lenehan's off-the-wall flair makes **Dolls Boutique** *(32b Westbury Mall, Clarendon St; www.dolls.ie; 672 9004)* one of our most playful and interesting designer shops, especially now that she's started her own line of evening and daywear using traditional materials like tweed and wool and favouring what she calls "old-fashioned shapes". There are no synthetic materials here, and local seamstresses do all the work.

Stepping into **Om Diva** *(21–22 George's Street Arcade; 087 410 1001)* is like taking a shot of consumer caffeine as you get a sudden jolt from the riotious colour and exotic fabrics. Owner and designer Ruth Niloinsigh works up her limited-run designs from offcuts of natural silks and cottons sourced from Thailand and India. Upstairs is Renewal, a trove of vintage fabrics and clothes refashioned by Ruth.

RE-FASHION Cheap, sustainable and lots of fun, charity and vintage shopping reverses any guilt one might feel about consuming. The key is to savour the rummage and the quest: take in the chatter and hum of the ultra-relaxed staff (definitely not on commission), try on something ugly from the 80s just for a laugh, and then browse at your ease in the hope of stumbling across a hidden gem. Shops vary a great deal in quality, with some of the top vintage stores getting very glitzy (and expensive), but even the humblest Capel or James St charity shop is capable of a delightful bottom-of-the-bin surprise.

Harlequin *(13 Castle Market; 671 0202)* piles a lot of clothes into a tiny space – women's upstairs, men's below – and is a great spot for a determined forage. High-quality gear from the 60s and 70s usually make for a rewarding dig.

A Store is Born *(34 Clarendon St; 285 7627)* has been appearing and disappearing every Saturday morning for decades now, and is a treasure trove of 20th-century classics for men and women with gorgeous cashmere cardigans, old-fashioned hats and colourfully printed silk scarves.

When it comes to charity shopping with a fashionista edge, **Ritzy Rags** *(25 Bolton St; 873 1855)* has long been a local standout. Friends of the Elderly have a gilt-edged connection with Les Amis des Petits Freres in France and get crates of second-hand French clothes shipped in twice a year. The warm and chatty Gretta Gray, who has managed the shop for nearly 20 years, knows her old designers and ensures an incredibly high quality of merchandise at prices that make you feel like you're ripping her off.

Of course, the folks behind **Oxfam** *(South Great George's St; 478 0777)* are old hands at charity shopping and there are several outlets around the city. The George's St store tends to get the tastiest items. Oxfam generally are choosy about what they take in donations, so the books, music and general clothing are usually good for a spirited rummage. The George's St store has vintage, a bridal section (by appointment only) and a window display that often features the best items and goes on sale at 10am every Saturday.

Nearby **Shebeen Chic** *(4 Great George's St; 679 9607)* first hit upon the idea of a fashion swap shop, which it stages every Saturday from 12 to 4pm. Walk in with a bag of unwanted clothes, and walk out with a new wardrobe – how's that for a bargain? No wonder this has become such a sociable hub for female (non-) shoppers.

Fashion ended at some point in the 1950s at **Jenny Vanders** *(Drury St; 677 0406)*, our local vintage clothing institution. It's been around for over 30 years now and specialises in antique jewellery and bags, with some pieces dating back to the 18th century. You won't find charity shop value, but the beautiful beaded ball gowns, exotic Victorian fitted bodices and handmade lace blouses will probably last a few more generations before they're done.

A friend of ours, Maeve, runs the fun and landfill-conscious **Vertigo Vintage** *(087 324 0252)* out of her own home in Phibsboro. Every couple of months she has a vintage party in her house where people can come and shop from her small but exclusive collection. She specialises in shoes, bags and jewellery and you just phone to find out when the next party is.

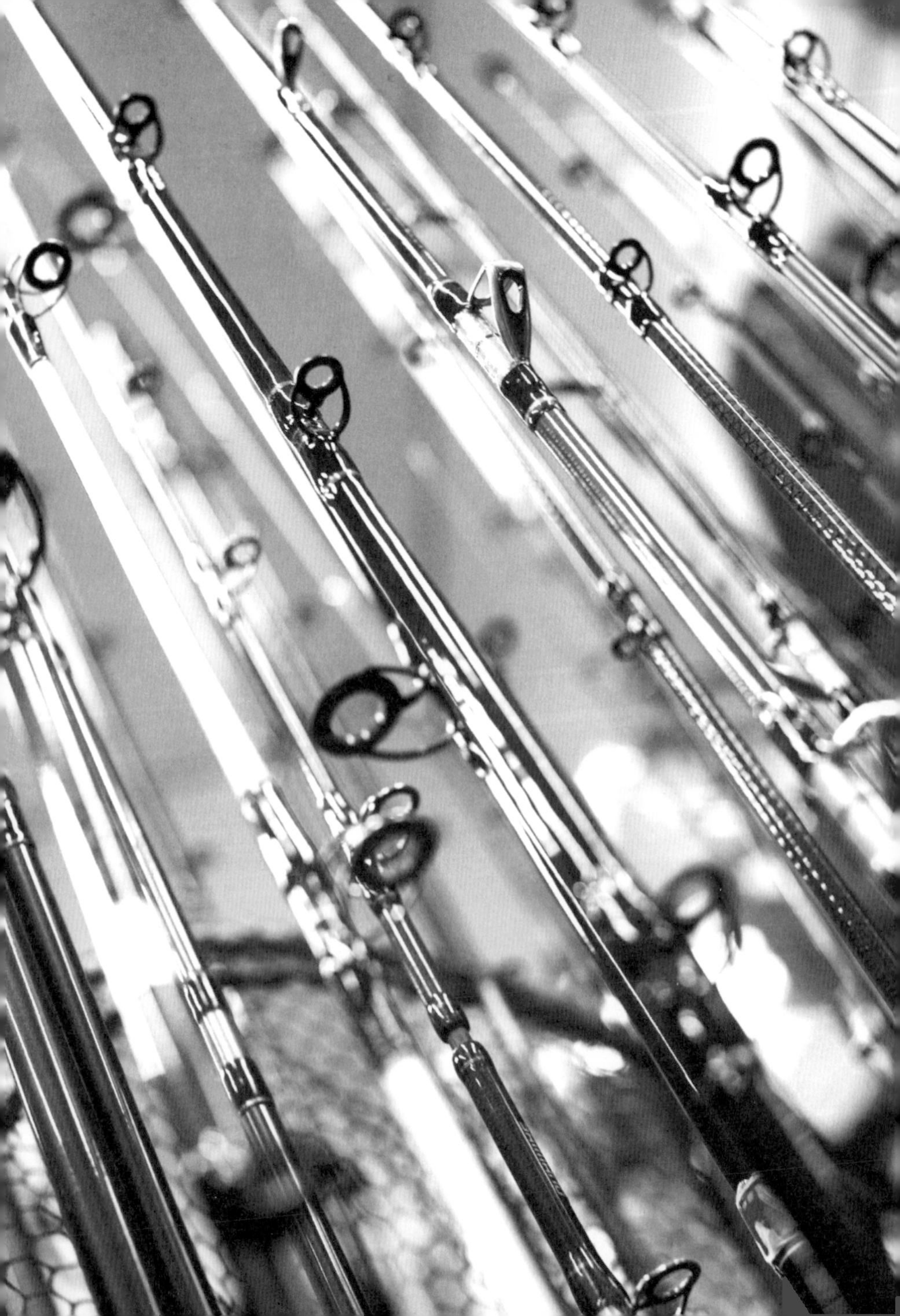

SPECIALIST STORES Dublin used to be full of small shops offering specialist products and personal service. The rise of suburbia and the omnipresent shopping mall killed many of them off, but we have rooted out some of the more inspiring survivors.

Young Christy Bird tells the story of how his grandfather and namesake, a retired widower with a family, opened his shop on Portobello in 1945. The first thing he sold was his own retirement clock. **Christy Bird** *(32 South Richmond St; www.christybird.com; 475 4049)* is Dublin's oldest furniture shop and was recycling household items probably before the word 'recycling' was invented. In the early days, "it was old, used black bikes" and a day hardly went by without some newcomer to the city going to Bird's for a cheap second-hand *rothar*.

They bought and sold whatever they could, including old skeletons (real ones) they got from students at the nearby College of Surgeons. The cheap, disposable, heading-for-the-landfill nature of modern furniture makes Christy grimace, and he prides himself on selling items that last. In fact, so sturdy are the second-hand and antique items here that they'll buy them back *again* when you're done with them. Christy's furniture has been used to recreate bygone eras on countless stages and film sets, and they can source antiques through contacts from all over Ireland.

We have vivid childhood memories of heading into **Rory's Fishing Tackl**e *(17a Temple Bar; www.rorys.ie; 677 2351)* with a pocket full of change on a Saturday morning and spending hours talking tackle, tench and line strength with the wonderfully knowledgeable and relaxed staff. Established in 1959, the family-owned business is a unique resource centre for all matters fish in Dublin.

Peeping in the door of **Murphy Sheehy & Co** *(14 Castle Market; www.murphysheehy.com; 677 0316)* is like discovering an Aladdin's cave of exotic fabric. Huge rolls of all colours are unceremoniously piled on top of one another and the place has the feel of a different era. In the same family and hardly changed since the 1940s, this has been the shop generations of sewers, tailors and seamstresses have turned to for something special. They specialise in Irish linens and wool and have a sideline in artist's canvases.

Yes, Kieran Byrne's **Square Wheel Cycleworks** *(21 Temple Lane South; 679 0838)* is Dublin's best bike shop and bike repair spot, but it is so much more. "We DO NOT repair cheap supermarket bikes," reads the sign on the counter, and on the wall a giant footprint of a Dublin driver sits next to a tiny one representing the carbon emissions of a typical cyclist. It's a hotbed of pro-cycle environmental activity and good vibes. They also sell specialised bikes sourced from small engineering companies, including some for people with physical disabilities.

Owners Dermot Carol and Brian Foley are not joking when they say they love the fact that **The Secret Book and Record Store** *(15 Wicklow St; 679 7272)* really is a bit of a secret. They don't advertise and like to keep the atmosphere unpretentiously chilled out and calm. Hidden away down a little corridor off Wicklow St, the shop houses a well-ordered and well-priced cavalcade of second-hand books, vinyl, CDs and DVDs. The owners are there most days and are always up for a natter about their chosen fields – Dermot is the book man, Brian does records.

MARKETS The boom years, when space was at such a premium, did for many of Dublin's better markets, including the Blackberry and Ivy. But the downturn has created more vacant spaces and the idea of affordable, sustainable market shopping is starting to blossom again.

One person's junk is another's treasure, for sure, and a colourful addition to Dublin shopping is the vibrant and slightly chaotic **Toe Jam Car Boot Sale** *(carpark of Bernard Shaw Pub, 11–12 South Richmond St; www.bodytonicmusic.com)*. Anyone can be a stallholder and it's a great excuse to clear the clutter from your life, make a few bob on the stuff you longer want, and mix with the greater community. Naturally, quality can vary, from top-notch vintage clothes and rare old albums, to some cheeky chappy trying to flog his dodgy old T-shirts (sorry about that). You never know what you'll find, from homemade cupcakes to a rare collection of academic books, a mountain bike going for a steal or even a bandy old Ford Fiesta. DJs provide music and people tend to get into a party mood with hot food straight from home and a few beers from the bar. It's usually on the first Saturday of the month but moves about a bit, so check the website for details.

Maybe it's a sign of the times, but at last Dublin can say it has a genuine flea market. You'll find a nicely random mix of attic clearers, young quirky designers and experienced marketers at the **Dublin Flea Market** *(Dublin Food Co-op, Newmarket; www.dublinfood.coop)*. It's on the last Sunday of the month and, like everything at the Food Co-op, there's a real bottom-up community feel to it, with an emphasis on recycling and reusing, and reasonable prices. We love the ultra-relaxed haggling that goes on with the very chilled-out stallholders.

The indoor **Blackrock Market** *(open weekends and bank holidays; Main St, Blackrock; www.blackrockmarket.com; 283 3522)* is full of little nooks, crannies and the sense that everybody knows one another.

The Collectors Shop is a highlight and owner James O'Brien describes it as "a hobby gone mad". He remembers when Dublin was full of old bric-a-brac markets like the Grafton Flea Market, the Dandelion, the Dún Laoghaire Harbour Market and the beloved Blackberry Market. His shop is of that old tradition, and you can get vintage stamps, coins, banknotes and, most strikingly, beautiful old postcards and pictures, many of them of Dublin. In all he has a collection of over 10,000 postcards of Ireland, some from as early as the 1880s. The last time we checked in, James had just received a complete album of Gallagher's Cigarette cards from the 20s, courtesy of a local woman who had just cleared her attic. Some of the stalls are a little tacky, but even that element has its charm.

A home-made fairy cake and a pot of strong tea at the Cup and Coin Cafe in the middle of the market is our favourite winter shop and stop spot. Cosy, relaxed and with delicious food, it subscribes to slow by hosting its own cooking classes and exhibiting local artists.

There's a lot of fake Gucci and cheap rip-offs at the **Liberty Market** *(Meath St)*, but it's a vibrant part of the inner-city community and has a few great stalls that make it worth a visit. The second-hand book stall is a piled-high, disorganised cave of old tomes at ridiculously cheap prices. The colourful wool stall and the noisy pet stall are as much unofficial advice centres ("How do you do a purl stitch?"

SELFRIDGES

or "How do you feed a budgie?") as they are businesses; there's a great place to buy sweet things for seasonal celebrations; and the tailor does the cheapest alterations in town.

Many a Dubliner must have pleasant childhood memories of the women who'd turn up at every major sporting event pushing their prams laden with frui' and chocola'. We might not do markets with the same panache as other European cities, but where else does the market come to you, literally, with individual stallholders just popping up wherever they please?

Lest we forget, Dublin's unofficial patron saint, Molly Malone, was a seafood stallholder. Mary Kavanagh isn't quite as old or buxom, but she's the longest surviving trader on famous **Moore St** and specialises in Dubliners' favourite fish, cod, ray and haddock, plus whatever else she can get her hands on out at the wholesale fish market in Blanchardstown. Mary and other sellers have to get out there before 5am and are usually still at their stalls 12 hours later – long days to be on your feet. Moore St is still a traditional fruit and veg centre and an influx of immigrant traders has reinvigorated the old strip.

What's sold on each street tends to reflect the character of each neighbourhood. Posh and romantic **Grafton St** is a natural fit for flower sellers, while workaday **Thomas St** tends to deal with essentials and the keenest prices. "Your boyfriend will love sliding these off your knee," said the woman hawking women's tights. This area seems to focus on accessories and household goods, with giant boxes of washing powder and toilet roll as cheap as chips. It's also the place to shop for the season, seeming to specialise in eggs at Easter, sparklers at Halloween and wrapping paper at Christmas. Traders in the shopping precinct of **Mary St** try to snaffle you with clothes, gifts and toys before you make it to the stores, while **Capel St** specialises in fruit.

You could do worse than to get out of the mall and spend a Saturday strolling between some of these stalls, taking in the air and having a laugh with the brazen vendors while you gather up the bones of a weekly shop.

BOOKS

For a city renowned for its literary greats, we really are lacking in good independent bookshops. There are, however, a few gems still quietly flying the flag.

A mysterious old hardback called *Vanishing Dublin*, with delicate watercolours showing prints and photos of corners of the city long gone, sits in the musty window of magical **Cathach Books** *(10 Duke St; www.rarebooks.ie; 671 8676)*. You could pass a pleasant hour browsing that one book alone, but Cathach is full of such rare local treasures; they specialise in older books of Irish interest, with an emphasis on 20th-century literature. It's a great place to pick up a pressie for a bibliophile, with first editions from many a famous local scribbler. The shop's name comes from the title of the oldest surviving Irish manuscript, *Cathach* or 'Battle Book', a psalter from the 6th century.

When they closed the old **Winding Stair** *(40 Lower Ormond Quay; www.winding-stair.com; 872 6576)*, many a Dublin slacker and student (if you can tell the difference) cried into their coffees. But fair play to the new owners, who've kept a downstairs bookshop and managed to retain the wonderfully chilled-out vibe. The selection is small but

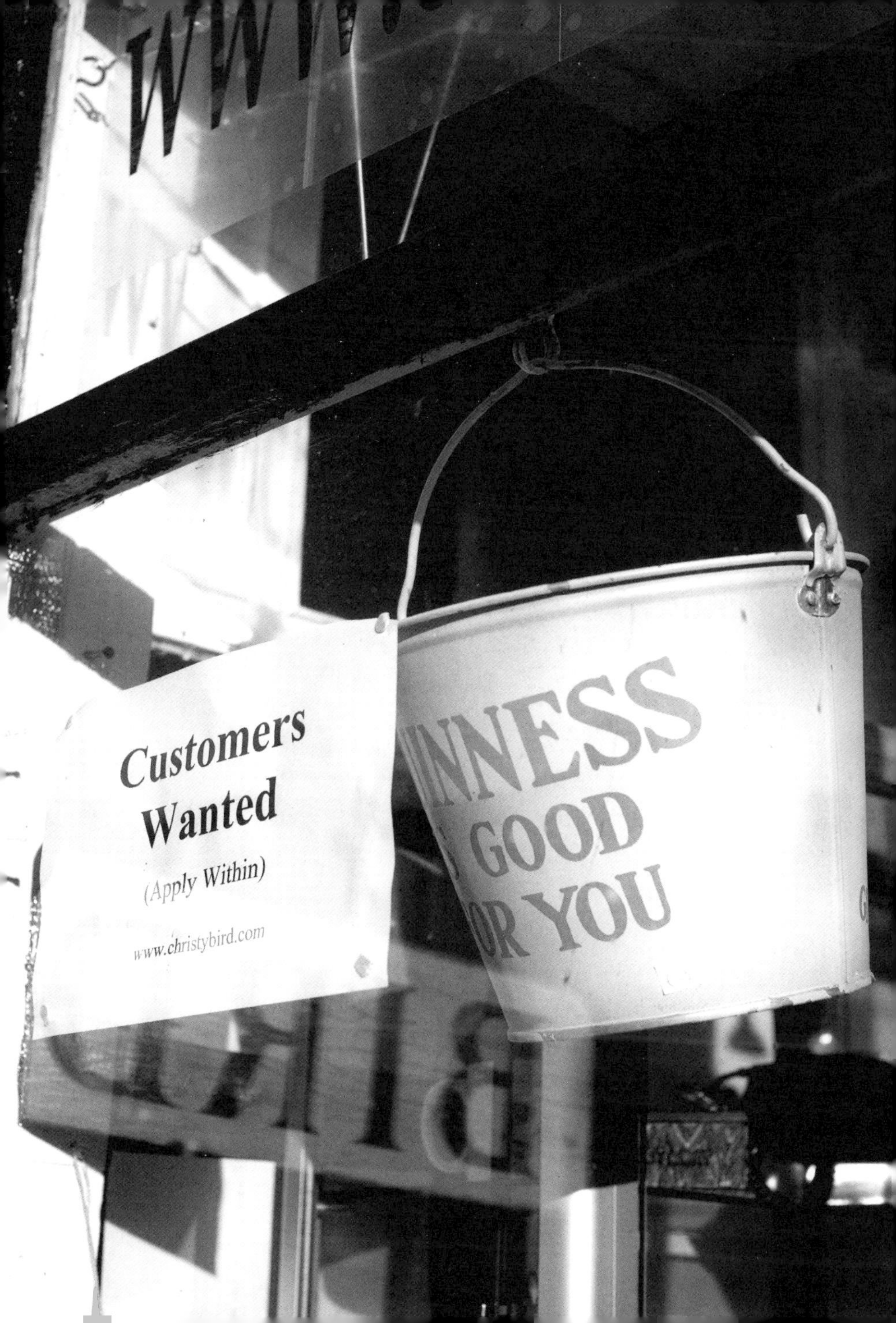

Customers
Wanted
(Apply Within)
www.christybird.com

selective, making it easy to navigate through and a great place to discover a new author. The staff recommendation shelf is always a good place to start, their Irish selection is strong, and they have regular readings.

Tucked away in George's Street Arcade, independent **Stokes Books** *(George's Street Arcade; 671 3584)* has been a favourite Dublin browse for nearly 25 years. Stephen Stokes entices market shoppers with some personally chosen books laid out on a table outside his shop. He specialises in Irish history and literature, with over 10,000 books ranging in value from five to five thousand euro.

As mainstream bookstores go, Dublin has a few that still manage to retain a good stock of character and literary charm. **Eason & Son** *(40 Lower O'Connell St; www.easons.ie; 858 3800)*, with its iconic blue and green paper bags, has been synonymous with books in the city since 1886. And Dawson St contains the most literary 100 square metres in Dublin, with highbrow **Hodges Figgis** *(56–58 Dawson St; 677 4754)* and **Waterstones** *(7 Dawson St; www.waterstones.com; 679 1260)* facing off in a perpetual cultural war from opposite sides of the street. Both have strong Irish sections. **Hughes and Hughes** *(Stephen's Green Shopping Centre; www.hughesbooks.com; 478 3060)* and **Reads** *(24–25 Nassau St; 679 6011)* are the best places to get a bargain on a new Irish literary hit.

The Shop that Time Forgot

You've surely noticed The Irish Yeast Company shop on College Green, the one that's always empty and has a simple, unadorned shopfront that looks like it was leftover from a period film set. Well, if you ever find yourself in desperate need of crimpers, figurines for wedding cakes, cake tins, petal powder, icing equipment or cake turntables, then this is the place for you. Dating from 1890, it's the second oldest shop in Dublin and walking inside the musty, faded interior is like stepping back through time, to an age when the city was full of family-run specialist stores that concentrated on one area of business and did it well.

Third-generation owner and sole employee John has stood in his shop and watched all the others disappear one by one. His eyes sparkle as he reminisces about "people crossing the road for the smell from the big vat of coffee beans being stirred in the window of Bewley's on Westmoreland St, stopping to watch the butchers at work through the window of Hafner handmade sausage shop on Talbot St, and hearing the knives being sharpened in Reads cutlery shop on Parliament St". Do you remember?

And by the way, for the pub quiz aficionados, the oldest shop in Dublin is said to be the Dublin Woollen Mills on the north side of the Ha'penny Bridge, which pre-dates the Irish Yeast Company shop by a few months.

Action at the Auction

I got my image of auctions from movies, and I always imagined them to be frenetically tense affairs where a few wealthy insiders know the ropes and an innocent lamb like me ends up scratching his nose and accidentally provoking a bidding war (then again, maybe the movie I was thinking of was *Mr Bean*). A trip to the 90-year-old Herman & Wilkinson *(www.hermanwilkinson.ie; 497 2245)* weekly auction in Rathmines soon set me straight and introduced me to the slow, traditional and sustainable pleasures of this old Dublin way of buying and selling.

The first thing I learned is that a good auction, a bit like a cricket match, takes a couple of days and breaks for lunch. Day one, a Wednesday afternoon, is the viewing. Potential buyers turn up, do a 'rekkie' of the goods on offer, and make notes of the lot numbers they might be interested in.

I'm a little intimidated when I slink into the large shed at the back of the auction rooms where, à la Aladdin's cave, all the treasures are on display. It really is quite a sight, like some giant had picked up a number of houses around the city, turned them upside down and shaken their contents out into this shed.

A random stroll brings me past a line of elegant antique armchairs; two tube radios from the 30s in their polished dark wood boxes; a very modern, good-as-new fridge–freezer; a wall of hanging paintings and photos that must span a couple of hundred years of Dublin art; an intact china tea set; and two long, elegant wooden skis, beautiful, old and useless.

The first thing to really grab me on a gut level is a simple, delicate doll's house. It's made of tin and painted in brightly coloured enamels, with a red roof that comes off and allows you access to the inside. I'm thinking niece, I'm thinking original Christmas present, I'm thinking brownie points and favourite uncle. A sticker on the side tells me it's lot number 165. "It's nice isn't it?" For a moment I think she's warning me off her patch and I make to get defensive, but regular Christina Giles quickly dispels any notions I have about the competitive nature of auctionistas. She spotted my slightly dizzy look from the other side of the shed, where she was browsing in a section of old lamps, and decided to take me under her wing.

"Decide your price," she tells me. "The porters will give you some idea if you ask, then work out your price and stick to it." I ask her about tomorrow, the dog-eat-dog arena of the auction itself, the frenzy I imagine is akin to the New York Stock Exchange floor five minutes before the bell. "Oh, don't worry, it's very relaxed," she reassures me with a smile. "There are lots of regulars and the banter is great. You could meet your future wife if you were looking."

I arrive Thursday morning, a little early in my eagerness, and get talking – it wasn't very hard – to amiable auctioneer David Herman. He's been in the business for over 40 years

and describes his weekly auction as "the ultimate recycling machine. When I started, there were 25 auction rooms in Dublin; now there are only two that really sell everything, like we do." David thinks people have a fear of auctions, "they think they're complicated and for the trade only. That's rubbish, they are for everybody, they're great fun and you'll get the best bargains in town."

But auctions take a bit of time, they can't be rushed, and he admits that his own grown-up children never come down and have turned their noses up at classic pieces of furniture he's snagged for them. The punters have arrived and I smile as they informally sit themselves down on the very chairs and sofas they'll be bidding on later. I join them on a particularly comfy rocking chair. David takes his place at a raised table and we begin.

He moves reasonably swiftly through the lots, but I notice the occasional pause and a few words of encouragement for any newbie who gets a little confused. The atmosphere is intimate and relaxed, with the occasional wry comment from the floor and most items sold without much bidding or competition. There's a bit more excitement when the name of an English monarch is placed before any item; Edwardian sideboards and Victorian tables are very popular. And man it is cheap! David starts a lot of the bids at as low as two euro! I lounge back in my forgiving chair (mustn't get seduced, can't fit another chair in tiny house) and enjoy the rhythm of the auctioneer's voice. I compare the different bidding techniques, from the teacher's-pet arm raised in the air to a very subtle, almost priestly nod of the head; no, not a nod, a mere flick. I'm impressed that all this great stuff – furniture, art, books – full of history and character, is finding a new home, rather that adding to some swelling dump on the city outskirts.

Lot 163, Lot 164... I nearly miss it, but suddenly the porter is holding up my beloved dolls house and I sit upright and prepare myself. "Fifteen euro, no higher", is my mantra. David begins the bidding at two euro, my arm shoots up like a crazy brownshirt. "Two euro to the writer," he grins in my direction. "Do I hear four?" I'm primed to react to the inevitable counter-bid. It never comes. "Sold for two euro!"

I head out into the daylight with my prize clutched to my chest and my heart still racing from the thrill of it all. One of the old hands smiles in my direction, and I get the feeling he's not impressed with my purchase. Beauty is in the eye of the bidder, I suppose, and that's the thing that separates an auction from any other shopping experience. It encourages us to express personal tastes and passions, and brings out the individual in us all.

Index

C

D

E

F

G

H

I

J

K

L

M

Q

R

S

T

U

V

W

Y

Z